Proceeds from the sale of this book are donated to the Westhill Central School District Educational Foundation, Inc. If you would like to know more about this organization, please visit
WesthillFoundation.com.

More on Coach Lukens' background may be found in the **Syracuse.com** archives under the following titles, all written by columnist Sean Kirst in January 2013:

Honoring a timeless coaching legacy:
Ed Lukens helped teens learn 'how to carry on'

Correspondence: Ed Lukens as great man, great friend, great coach

Ed Lukens and the Central reunion: At 91, a coaching model for tomorrow

WORDS OF WISDOM: FROM SKUNK CITY TO SKANEATELES

A Collection of Published Essays and Short Stories,
Supplemented with the Unpublished Writings of

Edwin W. Lukens

A Coach, Field Guide and Finger Lakes Fisherman;
A Founder of the Borodino Brain Trust and Holder of
Multiple World Records;
A Logger, Raconteur and World War II Soldier;
and
An All-around Role Model for a Four-Star General,
Financial Policy Advisor to Presidents,
an Unbeaten City Championship Basketball Team
and
Hundreds of Other Rummies.

Copyright © 2014 Edwin W. Lukens

Edited by David L. Reed, Esq.
and Lise M. Brown

Syracuse, New York

Cover photograph by Wynne Cotton.
Interior photograph courtesy of Westhill Central School District.

All rights reserved.

CONTENTS

I. STORIES, ARTICLES, AND MEMORIES   7

II. COACH LUKENS   209

III. SONGS   223

I.
STORIES, ARTICLES, AND MEMORIES

Edwin Lukens

OTISCO WATERSHED ADVENTURES

In the dim, distant past, an uncle of mine introduced me to the Otisco area. It was not Otisco Lake at first, but a small stream that still winds its way through Amber to the lake. A short distance upstream from town, a limestone face almost perpendicular exists. A growth of algae made it slippery and, sliding down into the deep pool below, gave great joy to a youngster who loved water and the challenge of the chute.

There was a place in Amber called "Heath's Grove," and it was my uncle once again who took me there. The grove was a place to picnic and swim. At water's edge a rope hung from a willow tree branch and with a healthy swing you could fly well out into the water.

Some years later a few fishing trips were made with a landscaper and worked for one summer. A rowboat was rented from Charlie Bouteille who ran a boat livery in Amber. We rowed across the lake to a spot near two white cottages. If my mind still serves me well, Wilson and Kemper owned those camps. Anyway, we drifted along the shore in about 15 feet of water using crabs for bait, and, low and behold, we actually caught fish. In truth, on those few excursions we did land fine catches of smallmouth bass. One Saturday afternoon I do recall three bass in the neighborhood of four pounds coming to the boat.

In the mid-1930s, the old Woodland Reservoir in Syracuse was drained for repairs. I lived nearby and what I saw when they netted fish and trucked them to Otisco and Jamesville Reservoir would astound you. Many times in tanks near bathtub-sized, only two lake trout were placed. The weight of the fish I would guess to be about 15 to 20 pounds. It was told the lake trout were taken to Otisco Lake and that may be true, because lakers were caught for many years after that time.

I knew a fellow who had a camp on the lake and he landed several lake trout.

Out of the Woodland Reservoir came an abundance of bass, perch, and whitefish as well. Where the whitefish went I do not know, but I think most of the bass and perch ended up in Jamesville Reservoir. It is amazing to understand fish traveling through pipes from Skaneateles Lake to the Woodland Reservoir, but all the species in that body of water were indigenous to the lake. The screens at the intake were made of heavy copper wire and holes only big enough to fit the end of your little finger in them. That would mean that the fish coming through were pinheads or minnows not much larger.

When I was young I tempted fate twice and suffered the consequences to some degree. I managed to break through the ice while skating and once while fishing. When it comes to thin ice on ponds and lakes only little boys and anglers tread there. Many lakes and rivers have been ice fished, Otisco included. Mainly pickerel, perch, and strawberry bass come to the hook and most were caught near the dam. Some years ago, norlunge, a cross between the northern and muskellunge, were introduced to the lake and quite a few have been caught in the lake and even in the outlet.

It has been said about the good old days that the older you get, the better they become. Memories aside, there is still the lift of heart in stream, lake, and verdant hillside in the Otisco valley. The Otisco watershed and lake were indeed valued friends through the years.

A SAD SONG

From the crest of the hill the hardwood-fringed, narrow dirt road fell away before me. In the distance, steep hillsides encroached on the narrow strip of water that was the lake's end. The miles ahead were swallowed in sunshine and the surrounding countryside, lavished by a late spring day, lay somnolent, peaceful, as it had almost for centuries. Breathing in the atmosphere, my mind lifted.

I strolled along, stirring little puffs of dust with each footfall, until I came to a three-tiered rail fence intertwined with rambling roses that surrounded a small two-story white frame house. I mounted the front stoop and rapped gently on the weather-beaten door. I heard Tom's gravelly voice say, "Come in. Come in."

I turned the knob, entered and confronted Tom seated in his easy chair, gray head pillowed.

He took a book from his lap, placed it on an end table beside him, rose haltingly and extended a gnarled hand. As I grasped it, he said, "It's been some time."

"Yes," I said, rather apologetically, "quite a while."

"I need a drink of water," he said. "Would you like one? Maybe you'd like a soda."

"No," I said, "Water will do fine."

I followed as he shuffled toward the kitchen. He let the water run for a moment, filled the glass, and handed it to me.

"You know," he said, "With all the beverages we have to choose from, sometimes we forget that water is good to drink."

Thirst quenched, he peered out the kitchen window, then turned to me and said, "Let's sit in the side yard and look at better things than that drab living room."

As we moved toward the yard, my eyes riveted on the stooped shoulders and leathery neck before me, tanned by a thousand and more suns. I thought of his 300-acre farm, now sold, and he alone and dying of cancer.

Before seating himself, he stood for a moment, eyes sweeping the far shore of the lake and the verdant hillside beyond.

"It awes me still," he murmured.

His eyes shone. He swallowed hard, bowed his head, and then sat down.

In previous visits he rarely mentioned his illness but no he seemed compelled to speak.

"Some of my friends want me to go someplace where I'll get some care, but as long as I can manage, I intend to stay here in this beautiful spot that's home to me."

He paused a moment, then continued. "Anyhow, if I moved away I'd probably die the sooner. You know my dyin' belongs to no one but me, so I wish they'd let me do it my way."

Evidently that was enough talk in that vein, for he abruptly switched the conversation.

"Clem phoned a few days ago. I asked him how the farm was goin'. He replied, 'It'll have to get along without me for a few hours. I was choppin' wood this mornin' and now my aches ache!'"

A wisp of a smile crossed Tom's drawn face.

"He sure has a way of puttin' things."

I knew that Tom and Clem were kindred souls even though they had many a skirmish. I think it kept them alive, sharpening their wits in a near lifetime as mile-apart neighbors.

Tom rambled on. "Last March I phoned Clem and asked for a weather report. He said, 'It rained early this morning; changed to snow an hour ago and if it stops I'll let ya know.'"

"At least it was up to date," I replied.

He reminisced further. "I asked Clem once why he still used a backhouse when he had money for indoor plumbing. 'Well,' he said, 'one morning I laid a cigarette down beside me and forgot it. A little later I smelled smoke. The cubbyhole was goin' up. Now that was one thing, but think of the disaster if the bathroom was in the house.' I didn't argue the point."

Tom laughed even though he was doing the telling of it. I joined in.

We were seated in old straight-backed chairs and I said, "These chairs seem real old, Tom, maybe antiques are worth something."

"I doubt that. They're old alright, but ain't worth nothin', just early American soapbox."

I smiled. It was good to see Tom more like his old self.

We talked for some time of many things out of the past until finally, with sun's light suffused in tree tops on western hills, I bid him goodbye, not knowing it was goodbye forever.

A SPARK AND A HOLOCAUST

On the shores of a beautiful lake near the Quebec-Labrador border nestled a small prospecting camp. Several whitewall tents with plywood sides and floors, drilling gear, two 20-foot freighter canoes, and a tractor composed most of the easily discernible equipment.

The sun warmed the land, unhindered by clouds, and a waking breeze swept away lake mist scrubbing the surface.

Less than a mile from camp, one of the crew was working with the tractor, towing windfalls from a drilling site. As he jockeyed his vehicle over a small mound, the muffler scraped dried caribou moss, and a piece was caught up. It then fell free, smoking like punk, to the forest floor. Almost instantly, the moss burst into flame, and before the driver glanced that way again, the fire, shouldered now by a strong breeze, moved swiftly across the patch of moss and into ground-hugging black spruce trees. The driver tried to stop it, but too late. It crowned in a matter of seconds. Knowing all was lost, the driver remounted his machine and raced down the trail.

The wind was blowing directly toward camp, and smoke started to sift through the tents. Thus warned, the men at camp radioed the floatplane base and quickly collected their few personal belongings. There was no time to dally, for they could feel the searing heat and knew that racing flames were close behind. They retreated from the onslaught to freighter canoes, which had been pulled up on the beach, and grasping gunwales carried them to water. Moving out into the lake a short distance, with eyes on the trail, they anxiously waited for their companion.

The flames were almost to the clearing where the flapping tents stood. Just before it reached them, the tractor with rider astride came charging out of the underbrush, the raging inferno snapping at his back. Straight through the camp and down the beach he flew, not slowing his machine in the slightest. He hit the lake in a shower of spray, and before the tractor rolled to a stop, he was in four feet of water. Quickly, one of the canoes moved in, snatched him from his perch, and then they paddled well out, away from smoke, spark and heat. No sooner had the man been taken aboard then the tents went up in flames. The heat close to shore became so intense that the large tractor tires protruding above the surface burst into flame.

A half-mile up the lake was a small island. There, the men gained a more permanent sanctuary and waited for the planes that would take them to a mining town less than 100 miles away.

From their vantage point, they watched as the camp was consumed in short order. The hungry flames moved around the end of the lake and angled up the slope on the other side, fanning out through verdant spruce and tamarack.

Soon, a beaver and otter float plane appeared low on the southern hills. The bush pilots bored in and, sighting the men, circled to check for obstacles that could impede landing, then dropped their planes. Off the island, shore water was deep, so canoes not needed for transfer were placed in the bush. With great relief, the men scrambled onto the planes, and although smoke and ash were drifting closer from flames moving along the near shore, the pilots taxied out and took off without a problem. They had escaped the holocaust.

In a matter of days, new equipment and supplies were garnered and a new camp was erected in the same area. However, the fire burned relentlessly on, and the damage to plant life and wildlife was appalling. The ravaged land would not see White Crowned Sparrow, Ptarmigan, or Caribou for years. Trees, which had been growing for 200 years and more, were destroyed by the thousands. Only blackened trunks remained; dark monuments of death and devastation. Three days after the camp burned, the fire was blazing on a front 30 miles away.

As all forest fires do, this one eventually came to a halt, extinguished not by man, but by heavy rains. Prospectors once again would probe the earth where scars were hidden from view, but the scars above ground would stand for decades.

BEHIND THE DOOR

"I'm Kirt Spilner," the man at the door said as he knocked the snow off his hat.

"My name's Ned. You're grandfather's brother, aren't you?"

"Yes and no. I'm his stepbrother." He brushed Ned aside as he stepped into the living room.

"How old are you, Ned?"

"Fourteen."

"I don't imagine you remember me. I came through here on another business trip about ten years ago."

"No, I don't remember, but Grandpa told me about you before he died."

"Died...when did that happen?"

"About a year ago. He fell down the cellar stairs; struck his head on the metal post near the bottom. Grandpa complained the house was too cold in the winter. He liked to go down and sit in his old easy chair by the wood heater where he would read and nap."

"Why didn't somebody tell me?"

"Well, Grandpa said he wrote several letters that you never answered, so I guess my parents didn't bother."

"The demands of my business afforded me little time. Where are your parents?"

"They went to dinner with friends in town; he told me they would be back by nine-thirty."

Mr. Spilner looked at his watch. "I guess I can wait that long. Ned, I wonder if I could trouble you for a drink. Would there be something around the house?"

Ned could smell liquor on him already, but he said, "I think father has a bottle in one of the kitchen cupboards."

Ned found the bottle and placed it and a glass on the kitchen table. He got himself a soft drink from the refrigerator and they sat for a time without a word passing between them; draining their glasses and Ned scrutinizing the bulbous-nosed, thin-lipped man before him.

Finally Mr. Spilner spoke. "You say your grandfather died from a fall. Did death come right away?"

"When he fell I don't exactly know. We found blood near the post. Evidently he lay there for a while unconscious. I came into the kitchen from my bedroom around nine that night and heard his steps on the stairs. He fell again against the cellar door there." Ned pointed to the door in the corner of the kitchen. "I can still hear his fingernails scratching on it. By the time I opened the door he was dead."

"That must have been quite a shock."

"Yes it was…and we miss him. Grandpa was real family."

Mr. Spilner's glassy eyes fastened on the door. "He died right there, you say."

"That's the spot."

Mr. Spilner poured himself another drink. "I guess that will be enough of this rotgut," he said, as he thumped the bottle down on the table.

Ned put the bottle back in the cupboard.

Mr. Spilner looked at his watch. "It's a few minutes after nine, about time for your parents to come home."

"Yeah, and maybe something else," Ned replied as he eyed the door.

"What do you mean by that?" asked Mr. Spilner.

"We don't really know. Lately we hear strange noises in the cellar around 9 o'clock, about the time Grandpa died."

"You don't believe in ghosts, do you?"

"I didn't until last night."

A muffled moan drifted up from the cellar.

Mr. Spilner looked at Ned, who was staring wide-eyed with horror at the door. A shuffling sound was followed by a methodical heavy step on the stairs and then scratching on the door. Mr. Spilner's chair flew back. He gained the living room, lurched through and out the front door, never looking back.

Ned, still seated at the table, watched the family cat and his grandfather come through the door. "Did you have a good nap, Grandpa?"

"Well, I did until Scooter jumped in my lap and woke me. What say we have some popcorn, Ned?"

"Sounds great, Grandpa."

CALL IT A WHITE LIE

Howard and Martha Granby lived on the edge of town. The adjoining land once farmed by Howard had been sold years ago when he went to work for a lumber company in a town twelve miles away. After twenty-eight years on the job, he retired. They were a spirited pair. Being hardworking, disciplined people endowed with a good sense of humor, affection and respect grew and flourished.

Just below their home, a town road angled off through the rolling countryside. It was a rutted, winding dirt road not maintained in winter, as there were no permanent residents living along its three-mile length. However, a few branches led to lakeside cottages, creating some traffic in summer months.

It was a favorite ride of the Granbys. They were akin to the land and all it encompassed. The serenity and strength of the everlasting hills . . . the iridescent beauty of the lake, lifted spirits. Often, Edward would back the old blue Ford out of the barn and they would sally forth in the sun and shadow, stopping occasionally to view the flora and fauna. They watched the thin veil of morning mist break clear of the lake and also gazed at the glory of sunsets; day yielding slowly and inevitably to oncoming night, at low western hills across the lake, and always on the great happenings, when the great skeins of geese would stop on the lake to rest as they shuttled to winter or summer quarters.

None can stem the tide of advancing years, and now in their late seventies, more than the normal tempering of old age was slowing the Granbys down. Howard was suffering from severe arthritis in his hands and Martha was blind.

Through the years they had shopped together at the one grocery store in town, usually driving in on a Friday afternoon. Now Howard went alone.

One day he said, "I'm going to walk."

She replied, "Take the car. The groceries will be too heavy for you."

"It's only a quarter of a mile and I need the exercise," Howard said. "Anyway, I can go in twice a week to lighten the load."

He never told Martha the real reason. His crippling arthritis made it difficult to drive and an accident in the grocery store's parking lot did not help matters.

Howard did not deny Martha her rides in the countryside, however, for she still enjoyed seeing them through his eyes. He would tell her in sharp description all that his eyes encompassed . . . bird life from song sparrow to great horned owl, sweeping on by on silent wings at dusk. Then too, the four-legged creatures . . . scampering chipmunk to the intent, quiet, white-tailed deer.

For two years until her death, like a tour guide, he recited in time schedule all the favorite spots where they had stopped so many times over the years.

Martha never knew that Howard deceived her. Not once in that two-year period did he travel the old road. Why? Because of his arthritic condition, the winding, narrow road, with its occasional car, posed a danger to Martha. So he drove the undulating perimeter of the fields near their home where farm machinery moving to and from the various plots had worn some semblance of a road. I like to think the Lord would pardon his deception.

After their last right together, the old Ford stayed in the barn, and in a manner of months, Howard too said farewell to green leaves and singing birds.

DON'T WAIT TOO LONG

With birth, death is also born.
None can escape. Some people endowed with rugged constitutions and a smile from lady luck live to a ripe old age. Others come to it before their time. Perhaps the majority will know it's coming…the shadow advancing until all is dark. But then death does not stalk, but strikes with one swift cruel blow, it leaves words unsaid, so many unfinished things lost like thistledown on a wayward breeze.

People cease to exist and so to some degree do others. None walk alone. The facets are a thousand-fold. The circle of influence – family, relatives, and friends – is all affected. Searing wounds that may never heal. The trauma makes life a shambles.

In a major disaster, like a school bus crash, young lives only started up the ladder come to a shattering end. A plane crashes. A ship sinks. The curtain falls on lives up and down the scale. Love, aspirations, the smiles and tears of a life unfulfilled.

Some may feel they never really said just how much a loved one meant to them. A firm shake of hand and a few words that are not superficial, but express in depth and measure the true worth of their existence. But it is too late now and the haunting thoughts linger through the years. The dead are monuments to yesterday, leaving loneliness resolute and determined.

I remember one tragedy…one loss. Three high school seniors were involved in an automobile accident. Two were injured but one of the passengers, Art Mathews, was killed in the grinding crash. Such a short walk in the sun. To Art's friends, and they were legion, he left a sadness that penetrated to the very core. He was a pillar of strength at home and an outstanding student athlete. More importantly, he was a fine, decent citizen of school and community.

When he walked up the street he always had a ready smile, a wave, and he was afforded the same warmth. Often he would stop and chat or lend a helping hand to lighten someone else's load. The neighborhood was a better place because of him and it would never be the same again.

In the classroom, student eyes came to rest on the empty seat; a voice stilled forever. Recollections shrouded in sadness flooded student minds. His smiling countenance missed from school corridors and leadership gone from school activities.

I remember his father watching the baseball games. He followed his son's exploits on the athletic field and gloried in his own way in Art's athletic prowess. The diamond where the home games were played had a grassy bank close by the third base line. From this vantage point he would watch Art pitch; eyes riveted on his son's every move. By mid-season Art had pitched two no-hitters and yet I never saw his father clap or show much outgoing emotion, but it ran deep. His hands closed in tense situations and eyes would glisten with pent-up emotion when a good job was done. The game over, he would wait patiently for Art until the clamor died, the equipment was picked up, and then walk home; their house was but a few blocks from the ballpark.

I have no recollection of his father placing an arm over Art's shoulder or heaping praise on him as they strolled along. In retrospect, I wonder if this became part of the problem. Perhaps Art's father felt he should have said more, patted him on the back, clasped his hand.

Certainly I do not know what thoughts came to his father after Art's demise. He was the center of his father's universe, an integral part of the family, and now the chain was broken. It was too much to hold. Art's death left a permanent void…too permanent. For his father nothing transcended the moment I never saw him smile again. He was forever lost in a dream world with a treasury of bright memories and future hopes that dissolved in a perpetual fog. To drown his sorrow he turned to the bottle and in a few short years he joined his son. Life does not always go on.

It happened long ago and yet the durable impact has marched down through the years. Art is still missed.

I miss him, too.

FATHER'S DAY

My father was born on April 7, 1896. Few people knew when he was born, for he never became a prominent figure. At first, he was a designer of chinaware; later, he did drawings for television and radio.

Forty-five years laboring over a drawing board should have brought him the fruits of victory earned in a multitude of battles through troubled years. He served in World War I, fought depression and company failure, the problems of a new job, and World War II. However, in the 20 years that followed the last Great War, mother's long illness denied much more than meager savings.

Now he lies under a small gravestone in a quiet cemetery, a monument to yesterday, but not entirely – he lives in my memory forever, leaving loneliness that transcends all. I remember him for what is honest, unselfish, kind…for all that is bright, cheerful, yes, good in this world. I lost some of it when he passed away.

Most people would judge him a common man. To me he was an uncommon one. Concessions were not made to his code of ethics and many of the greatest lessons in life were his heritage.

Not until my brother and I were up in the teens did the luxury of a car come our way. Therefore, as youngsters, most of our living was done in close proximity to our home. Range depended on strength of leg. Living less than a mile from the edge of town, we were drawn to the countryside to picnic or wander fields and woodlands.

All trips were a special adventure. Father liked the laughing streams, quiet ponds, and his deep interest in nature's scheme created a love of wonder in us. We observed the changing seasons: flights of Canadian honkers, robins, and horned larks; later, song sparrow and orioles. Animal life from mouse to deer as well as plant life; hyacinth, dogtooth, violet, trillium, the noble red oak, and sugar maple. He knew them all, and when our wanderings led to a shadowed brook on a summer's day, we waded the cool clear water, watched water spiders skitter on the surface and crayfish dart backward to safer haunts. In winter, flights of crows to rookeries in the pines and tracks of pheasant, rabbit, and fox in fresh snow intrigued us.

In winter's snow, my father died. The first spring comes and as I sit quietly in the old house, a soft breeze rustles curtains of southern windows carrying fragrant scent of lilac and my thoughts focus on my father who planted them on another spring day long ago. Incidents of boyhood, a thousand fond recollections materialize from the mists of time. The joy of meeting him on return from work as he alighted from trolley and together we talked of days events as feet slapped the time-worn red brick sidewalk that led down to our home.

Memories of father pulling me on a sled of another generation. Higher than most sleds, with little metal except for runners, and hard to steer, it nevertheless had ample room for the two of us to coast the slopes above our home. In warmer weather, hikes to an old reservoir to swim, and when luck was with us, catch a few fish for dinner. Then too, excursions were made to the park, father leading the neighbor's kids as well as my brother and me for a lesson in football or baseball.

There were also lessons of a more subtle nature – chores, as father called them. We learned of life by participating in it. Floors were scrubbed, snow shoveled, groceries carried home. Father dug a vegetable garden, laboring with a fork. Brother and I helped plant and tend it, taking on the burden of family sustenance and thus became providers and caretakers at an early age. It also gave us mutual concerns to talk about.

When the long winter was upon us, father was the first one up to shake down the coal furnace and draft it, so we arose to rooms with some semblance of warmth. Arriving at the breakfast table, we found oatmeal merrily plopping on the stove, ready for consumption. He was the spark, the catalyst that kept alive our dreams and aspirations.

Years later when my brother, who was severely wounded, and I returned from service, he still rose to greet sun or winter's dreary shadows to start us off with a decent breakfast. He had consistency of purpose that denied weather and more than minor ills. Many times he struggled when bed should have been the accepted fact. When mother would ask, "Why are you going to work?" he would answer, "I've got a job on the board."

In my childhood, mother's illness prevented her from undertaking anything but light tasks and she never fully recovered. Father never wavered. He accepted the extra load until the end of his days.

Rarely did he raise voice or hand, but I remember a time in the thick of depression, when one Sunday after Church I wandered to a nearby stream and, aided by a sapling, tried to pole vault across. The pole sank deep into mud bottom and I landed short, soiling my best pants and shoes. I'm sure father admired my spirit, but he would little afford such mishaps, and the laying on of hands was reluctantly administered. I don't know if I fully understood such measures at that particular time, but I soon realized he was honest in his actions and if I got mad at him, I shamed myself.

Just before entering service during World War II, I planted a maple tree in the front yard. As I traveled around Africa and Italy, mail would arrive from mother with mention that, "Pop is taking care of your maple tree," and so he did. On returning I found it had grown considerably. A great change had also taken place in father. Facial lines were deeper and dark hair and moustache had become steel gray.

Although a quiet patriot, he was always ready to display the flag with reverence and care. The family flag had 45 stars. It was hung from the front porch roof and nearly reached the ground. The task finished, he would pause to survey it for a moment, not saying a word, and then, with a nodding salute, would turn to the cares of the day.

Strangers made him self-conscious, but among family and friends he regaled all with stories from the past of light-footed lads with lighter hearts. His ready smile and breath-catching laugh leaves a durable and lasting impact.

An inoperable brain tumor caused his death. In little more than two months he was gone. Ever the same, during that period he knew the inevitable and yet he did not dwell on the long voyage that was to come. Companion with life, through life, he now fought for it. It was a crooked game. To the bitter end his pride would not allow him to wallow in self-pity or bring grief to others. No word of this nature escaped his lips. Perhaps he was still teaching us a lesson: how to die – the man that was my father, my friend.

And when he died, only then did I feel the full weight of him.

I REMEMBER AUNT ROSIE

When I came into the world, Aunt Rosie was there, for I was born in grandmother's house with its white columns and sharp peaked roof, situated on the crown of a hill where it commanded a sweep of rolling fields and wooded hillsides.

Aunt Rosie, my great, great aunt, lived with grandmother for almost forty years but the distance being less than a mile to our home, she lived at the heart of both households.

Mother was frequently bedridden and on many of these occasions Aunt Rosie took over, keeping our house on an even keel. She was always first up to start us off with a healthy breakfast and a warm smile. Housed in her hazel eyes was a constant gleam reflecting the fire within and oh, what a fire!

In the dark Depression years she lifted spirits by creating culinary magic that seemed to come out of the air, as well as little treats that originated in her change purse. Her income was derived from small gifts tendered by her own relatives. Mother tried to convince her to spend the money on her own needs, only to be told, "I will spend it as I see fit." A smile was on her lips but Mother knew she meant it, so her selfless acts continued.

Aunt Rosie was a thread over five feet, thin, wiry, and weighed only 88 pounds. Her back was hunched with a permanent set, but in that thin hunched frame, she carried great pride and dignity.

How she remained so kind and cheerful over the years is still a mystery to me. It was more surprising considering her early life. At the age of twelve she was working long hours, six days a week, in a factory; a better name would be "sweatshop." Marriage was attempted but her husband entered into the world of the bottle and wandered off. There were no children. Possibly that is why she loved all children the more.

Many years passed before Aunt Rosie joined grandmother in a small town in New Jersey. This happened soon after grandmother's husband died, when my mother and her younger sister and brother were still small. It was a span of years before grandmother married again, and during that time Aunt Rosie's artistry with the needle created most of their clothing. She also cooked for family and several boarders. The attic of the large wood frame house was fixed to accommodate the children, and boarders took over most of the five upstairs bedrooms.

She never told me of past heartbreak in earlier years. When I did hear, it came from my mother. We were living in upstate New York then. I was in my teens and Aunt Rosie near the end of her days. As I looked back, my admiration grew. She believed life was wonderful and lived it that way day on day, totally immersed in the well-being of others, enjoying every moment and attacking each task with an evenness of performance that transcended all things.

When my brother and I had petty differences or hurts to administer to, she gave quick response and we were the better for it afterward. A very special understanding was hers. Discipline was tendered with warmth. You soon realized that to disobey Aunt Rosie only shamed yourself. Usually her crooked forefinger shaking in your face and a "We shan't do that again," was enough.

Many times she said to me, "Even in you there is some good. I am not sure what it is but we will find it." Then she would smile, place a hand on my head, and muss up my hair. Another statement often directed to me was, "You are full of the devil, boy, but I am going to see to it that you come out alright." Sometimes I think that was the only task she undertook that failed.

One day with housework done at grandmother's, she struck out for our house. Directly in our line of flight lay a reservoir. It had a sidewalk around the top and to gain it a steep, high terrace had to be surmounted. On arrival I was astounded to see her drop on all fours. I offered assistance but to no avail. She scrambled up and stood at the top, triumphant; her body seemed to straighten and she looked all the more imposing with abundant white hair piled high on her head. She was 91 at the time, and what an independent lady. I asked why, with all the cooking and housework at grandmother's, she came to help us. I am not certain I understood her answer then, but I do now.

"Well," she said, "I don't have much money, a little change in my purse, no trinkets of value, but I am rich in people to do things for."

She was grateful for a roof over her head, a warm bed, meals, and friends.

Deeply etched in my mind is the story she told me one beautiful summer's day while we sat on the roadside bank in front of grandmother's house, a breeze rustling the leaves of the giant maple that towered above us. It was of Abraham Lincoln; how in her youth, she heard him speak and when he finished she had pressed forward and conversed with him. I thought of the history encompassed in her years and how young the country was . . . Aunt Rosie spoke to Abraham Lincoln, and I to her.

Like most youngsters, I had restless periods when body and soul were not occupied. If Aunt Rosie figured she could spare the time, we went on "safaris," as she called them, little sojourns to the fields across the way; or beyond to a pond in the fold of the hills, where cattails nodded and water spiders skittered on the surface. She also lectured on the development of the frog, pointing out with a stick the various stages from egg through tadpole to maturity.

In her 94th year, Aunt Rosie passed on. She was doing what she had always done, helping with the tasks of the day. She started for the cellar, tripped on her long skirt, and fell headlong down the stairs, breaking several ribs and her collarbone. She lingered on for sometime, but her body could not repair the damage.

I do not remember her going to church during my time. The household got religion while she took care of the house. Aunt Rosie's religion was a permanent affair, constant as her reading of the Bible - daily. If there is a heaven and a hell, Aunt Rosie is not sweating, unless it is because she is doing some work for the Lord.

Once in a gathering, when asked which side of the family she was on, she laughed and replied, "I am not on any side, I am neutral."

The simple fact was that she stood for what was right.

Of all her qualities, perhaps the one that rises above the rest was her constant dedication to every task and therefore a dedication to life. She did not take time to dwell on past defeats or tragedies, but always moved on.

In my mind's eye I see her once again, a little white-haired pixie with smiling countenance and dancing eyes, peeking over gold-rimmed glasses. I remember her for what is honest, unselfish, kind . . . for all that is bright, cheerful, yes, good in this world.

When she died, a little light departed from my days.

IT AFFECTS ALL

Recently, I was given a copy of the 9/11 Commission report. It was an exceptionally sad treatise on an appalling disaster. The great loss of life and heroic efforts shake you to the core. Intertwined in the report are so many loose ends that hopefully could have stemmed the tide if more cooperation among organizations with he the disseminating information had taken place.

The catastrophe that befell us on Sept. 11 had far-reaching repercussions. A friend of mine who was involved with me in a teacher-coach situation at a high school, has a daughter who lost a husband in the World Trade Center. One of my former athletes, now an attorney, mentioned in a letter that a fellow living next door had perished in New York City.

I was rocked by the Pentagon crash as well. Some months before Sept. 11, 2001, an article appeared in the Syracuse paper concerning a brigadier general in charge of security and intelligence throughout the Army. He was a fine student and good athlete on teams that I coached. He had mentioned me to a reporter, and so I was contacted and questioned regarding the general. A few weeks after the article was published, I received a letter from him that mentioned responsibilities during his career and stated he had been raised in rank to major general.

The reason I mention the general is in relation to the plane crashing into primarily Army offices in the Pentagon. After the dust had cleared, I called the local office of Rep. James Walsh and was given a number in the Pentagon. I called immediately and a very polite and helpful person quickly checked the missing list and then followed with an accounting of the injured. A considerable weight was lifted off my shoulders when I was told my friend was all right.

I am content in knowing that a good man is still in charge of the security and intelligence in the Army.

MRS. DURGAN'S SALVATION

"Why is Mrs. Durgan so crabby, Mom?" Mrs. Arden turned from her dishwashing chore and addressed her twelve-year-

old son. "Tom, you shouldn't say that. Mrs. Durgan isn't crabby."
"Then why does she holler at me every time I get near her lawn?"

"You probably do more than get near it, Tom. Wouldn't 'cross it' be more like it?"

Tom fidgeted with his blue baseball cap and looked down at his feet as if to blame them for his travels across Mrs. Durgan's yard.

"Even if I did cross it, I didn't hurt it any."

"Maybe you didn't, but Mrs. Durgan isn't herself since her husband died, so if she wants it that way, you keep off."

"Okay, Mom."

Tom turned and flew out the side door into the sunshine of a beautiful spring day. A wisp of breeze gentled the new bright green leaves of the maple tree in front of the Arden home. From a secluded perch high up in the branches, a robin sang. All seemed right with the world.

Billy Sanders was presently whistling his way down the street. Billy waved, broke into a gallop, and arrived out of breath, but able to convey his message.

"Let's go over to Horton's Pond and catch some frogs."

"Okay. Better tell our mothers we're goin'. Meet you here by the maple tree."

With that, Billy wheeled and headed up the street.

The joyous trip to the pond was not to be, for fate was to play its hand. As the boys parted, Mrs. Durgan emerged from her door and proceeded to sweep the sidewalk. She was bent by the weight of sixty-eight years and even more by her husband's passing. She swept the front walk, impervious to the beauty of the spring day – of the green leaves, the fragrance of blooming lilacs, and singing birds.

Tom, smiling with anticipation of adventures to come, was first to arrive at the maple tree. He eyed a low branch and pulled himself up into the cool green sanctuary. He climbed a bit further. Below, he heard the sound of Mrs. Durgan's broom scratching the sidewalk. He wondered why she scolded Jimmy Hazelton when his baseball rolled into her yard a few days ago. He was aroused from his thoughts by the sound of Billy's feet.

Tom started down but, in his haste, lost his footing. He struck a branch with his chest and then landed on his back in the grass below. Billy stopped short, dumb-founded by the proceedings. Mrs. Durgan, nearly through with her sweeping, heard Tom's deep groan as he struck the limb and fell to the ground. She stopped her chore, took in the situation, and immediately dropped the broom. Billy, gaining control of himself, blurted out, "Tom fell out of the tree! Somebody help him!"

The only somebody within sight or sound for the moment was Mrs. Durgan, who already was ambling across the street as fast as she could go. Tom, stunned but not unconscious, was groaning and trying to rise. Mrs. Durgan knelt down and placed a hand on his shoulder.

"Don't try to get up, Tom. Billy, tell Mrs. Arden that Tom fell out of the maple tree. Control yourself boy. Don't scare her half to death."

Billy ran to the side screen door, opened it and called Mrs. Arden. Mrs. Arden, still at her kitchen chores, recognized his voice. "What is it, Billy?"

"Tom fell out of the tree but I don't think he's hurt too bad." "Good Lord!" Mrs. Arden exclaimed, and pushing Billy aside, hurried to the front of the house. Mrs. Durgan, comforting Tom as best she could, looked up as Mrs. Arden approached. "He seems to be doing pretty well but I don't think we ought to move him."

Tom's mother dropped down beside him and grasped his hand.

"Are you alright, Tom?"

"I guess so, Mom, but my chest hurts."

Mrs. Durgan spoke. "I think we had better take him to the hospital. I'll call an ambulance." Mrs. Arden said, "Billy, take Mrs. Durgan to our phone. It's closer."

Billy obliged and after the call was made they returned to Mrs. Arden and Tom, whose face was now contorted with pain.

"I think you're hurt more than you say, Tom," his mother said. "We're going to the hospital and let and doctor look you over."

The ambulance arrived. Tom was gently placed inside and taken to the hospital, where he remained for several days, with two broken ribs.

Billy's mother decided to have a little neighborhood coming home party for Tom in her backyard, weather permitting. Tom's friends and their mothers and fathers were invited, and last, but not least, Mrs. Durgan. She accepted after Mrs. Arden's gentle prodding. The neighbors pitched in to make the party a success.

Finally the day arrived. On a morning that matched the occasion, Tom was brought home. The party began early that evening. Tom was told they had been invited to join the Sanders family for a barbecue. Dinnertime came and Tom and his mother started up the street.

"Where's Dad?" he asked.

"He went on ahead." Tom seemed satisfied.

As they rounded the corner of the Sanders' house, Tom was astounded to see over thirty people gathered there.

"Why are all these people here?" But before his mother could say a word, the answer came in wave a humanity that surged forward to grasp Tom's hand and tell him how glad they were to see him home again.

Eventually the greetings subsided. The neighbors began to visit again, and then dine on the savory dishes prepared by loving hands. With the meal over the visitations went on. Tom, seated on a lawn chair with mother and father, was still the center of attraction, but the get-together was beginning to encompass more than him. Mrs. Jordan wished Tom well and thanked him for his errands run on her behalf. She moved away and in the lull that followed, Mrs. Durgan walked hesitantly toward them and lowered herself gingerly into a nearby chair. With head somewhat bowed, she looked over her glasses and spoke haltingly to Tom.

"I'd like to thank you for what you did for me."

Tom, somewhat astonished, blurted out, "For what I did for you? It was the other way around."

"Maybe so boy, but something else happened that has meant a great deal to me." Mr. and Mrs. Arden listened intently as she continued.

"When my husband died, it was almost unbearable, and in the months that followed, I was very depressed and didn't want anyone to bother me. I lost contact with the good people on the street. I supposed I'm making an excuse for being impolite and even mean to young and old alike, but –"

Mrs. Arden broke in and tried to put Mrs. Durgan at ease. "You don't have to apologize. We understand and wish to thank you again for your quick action when Tom had his accident. The doctor told us that any movement of his broken ribs might have caused internal bleeding. Tom told us how you restrained him when he tried to get up. Your understanding of the situation was deeply appreciated. Actually, this get-together was for you as well as Tom. I wonder, Mrs. Durgan – would you join us for dinner next Tuesday?"

"I'd like that very much, Mrs. Arden."

The party went on for some time. Tom's accident, although dark at its inception, became a beacon in the end, for it brought all the neighbors closer together, and it opened up Mrs. Durgan's world once again to the warmth of good friends and a revered place in the neighborhood.

MY WONDERFUL PILOT FRIEND

It was some time ago that I first ventured into the Canadian wilderness. With the wanderlust in my veins, I extended my reach northward in the years that followed. Eventually floatplane flights were made to rivers in the Hudson Bay area.

In an air station where I boarded planes, I met Reg Philips who was both pilot and manager of the operation. Later he switched to another air outfit that was based along the Quebec-Labrador border. I followed him there. A long relationship evolved and I thoroughly enjoyed his companionship whenever we were together.

In the early years of my escapades into the Quebec-Labrador area, the planes out of Montreal were turbo-props that handled the dirt runway at flight's end in good style. Later with a paved runway the jets took over.

As I was a teacher-coach at the time, I had summers free. On one occasion after being flown out from a camping trip, Reg said, "How is it you can come out of the bush as good as you went in?" Then he said, "How would you like to work summers guiding parties at our lodge and possibly in our out camps too?" It didn't take long to answer in the affirmative.

I not only worked as a guide for a time, but also did quite a bit of flying to check rivers, primarily for out camps. If the rivers had an abundance of fish such as brook trout, Atlantic salmon, landlocked salmon, arctic char, and lake trout, and if navigable to some degree, a camp might be installed.

Through warmer months, pilots were busy from sunup till dark, moving personnel, supplies, and equipment to fishing and hunting lodges and prospecting camps. To keep up with the schedule, Reg would often leave someone to cover the operation shack and take to the air.

Reg was one of the most interesting persons that ever came into my life. His sense of humor transcended all problems of management and flying. Concerning the weather in the area, Reg figured they had 10 months of winter and two months of poor sledding. I guess that was on the mark because we had snow in August, and I remember a 17-degree day and an inch of ice in a water bucket outside my tent.

Reg had been involved in all kinds of missions including servicing early warning stations along the north coast. He made the statement that there are old pilots and bold pilots, but there are no old bold pilots. The airline that flew out of Montreal to a point near the floatplane base would give you a snack in transit. That would be a sandwich, and it often seemed they were on the stale side. I thought they might be leftovers from previous flights. Reg explained it this way: "Some of the sandwiches had more flying time than the planes."

The Beaver was the main workhorse among floatplanes. When I last worked in the Canadian wilderness, that plane had not been made for 20 years or more. The fuselage was DeHaviland and the motor Pratt and Whitney. The air outfit was picking these planes up all over the world. I remember they garnered several from a United States military post in Germany and even one in Australia. Reg said he noticed the paint had flaked off one of the planes recently found, and the insignia of the Lafayette Escadrille could be seen. That gave me a good laugh. I'm sure it was a little exaggeration as the Lafayette Escadrille was a World War I squadron.

One afternoon while I was in the operation shack, a fellow came in and started to press Reg about getting into a lodge some 130 miles away. The weather was bad with overcast skies down on the mountains. Without instrumentation you could not fly, and no plane had instrumentation. If you went up above the cloud cover you might kiss a mountain coming down through it.

The guy kept pressuring Reg and finally he told him we have all kinds of planes, but I haven't got one with a propeller that can chew granite. I guess that soaked in because he didn't pester Reg again.

I have kept in touch with Reg, but now it is a note or Christmas card. I miss the camaraderie and his smiling countenance.

REFLECTIONS

Mr. Harding closed the door on the noisy machines and mounted the stairs. As he swept through the outer office he noticed a thin young man seated on one of the straight-backed wooden chairs. He wore a threadbare brown jacket open at the front and on his lap, a cap and mittens. Mr. Harding frowned at his secretary and said without stopping, "Will you come to my office, Mrs. Lowery?"

She rose, followed him through the door and closed it softly behind her. He walked around his desk; stood facing her and said, "Who is that ragged kid sitting out there?"

"His name is Ed Lukens and…he's looking for a job."

"A job! We haven't any openings. We're having a hard time keeping our present help busy."

"I told him we weren't hiring but he wanted to speak to you."

"And you consented? Mrs. Lowery, I have enough to do without taking time to talk to some ragamuffin."

"I don't think he's a 'ragamuffin,' as you put it. He seems like a decent boy. Don't judge a book by its cover."

Mr. Harding stared at her for a moment then replied, "After I make a phone call I'll let you know when to send him in."

Mr. Harding picked up the phone. Mrs. Lowery wheeled and returned to her desk. As he finished the call he was distracted by the whisper of granular snow against the large window behind him. He stood gazing at the snow-covered street below. A youngster on the far side pulling a sled loaded with newspapers caught his eye, and the scene held him. He watched the lad straining duck-footed like a skater, with boots too big for his size, digging in to keep the sled moving.

The boy stopped to rest in front of Schuler's Bakery. He tossed the rope over his papers and drew a mittened hand across his nose. Mr. Harding smiled as the boy stepped to the window, pressed his face to the glass and peered at the baked goods in the cases just inside.

A shiver went up Mr. Harding's spine. He was watching himself over 30 years ago. So many times he had pulled the almost-all-wood sled of another generation along the same route, peddling the evening paper. He could feel the string of the granular snow on his face and a twinge in his left shoulder from tugging the sled into motion after each delivery. Once again the smell of the coal fires was in his nostrils and then the tantalizing aroma of baked goods as he neared the bakery. And he remembered the brown jacket he wore with the tattered wristbands – a hand-me-down from his brother. He also recalled the high-top boots, two sizes too large, with tissue paper in the toes, tissue paper that stopped the feet from sliding. It eliminated some of the blisters and insulated toes that, for the most part, were covered by white cotton 5-cent and 10-cent store socks.

Swirling snow fingered the windowpane. The boy had disappeared around the corner. Mr. Harding snapped from his reverie. He flipped a switch on the intercom and said, "Send in the young man, Mrs. Lowery."

Mrs. Lowery appeared in the doorway. "This is Ed Lukens," she said, and closed the door behind him.

They shook hands and Mr. Harding said, "Have a chair."

I seated myself, placed cap with mittens inside, on my lap. "I…I'm in need of a job, Mr. Harding. I've got to help my mother support the family."

Mr. Harding winced. For a moment he scrutinized the boy, the lock of brown hair that covered the right side of his forehead, hazel-green eyes and a tattered brown jacket. "There's an opening in the shipping department if you want it."

"I sure do, sir. Thank you."

"Tomorrow morning see Mr. Henson. He's in charge." He turned on the intercom. "Mrs. Lowery, come in here."

As she entered, Mr. Harding addressed her. "We're going to put Ed to work. Will you take care of it?"

"Certainly, Mr. Harding."

"Thanks again, Mr. Harding," I said as I walked out.

Mrs. Lowery, with hand on the doorknob, peeked over her glasses and smiled at Mr. Harding.

He frowned at her and said, "That will be all, Mrs. Lowery."

She closed the door.

Mr. Harding looked out the window at the falling snow and smiled.

THE DREAMER'S HANDS

"Remember, Tom, I don't want you visiting old Ben Hardridge. He filled your head with so many stories last summer that I never heard the end of it. They're a lot of baloney."

"How can you say that, Dad? You don't know if they're true or not."

"He couldn't have done all those things in a hundred years."

Tom looked at his mother in the front seat, hoping for support, but she said nothing.

"Mom, do you think what he says is a lot of baloney?"

"Well, Tom, he does tell a great many stories — "

Tom's father cut her off. "They're fairy tales. I don't want to hear any more about it and that's final."

His mother bowed her head for a moment and then said, "I'm sure your father's right. They're probably fairy tales."

Tom swallowed hard. He pulled at the peak of his green baseball cap and slumped down in his seat. He thought of Ben, his little cottage by the cove, and how they had so much fun together when they vacationed there last August.

If father had his way, he would hear no more of Ben's exploits on the high seas. The thread of one invaded his mind. He could see Ben as a cabin boy on a whaler, rescuing the captain, swept overboard in a raging storm. For a time he lost himself in reverie.

It was mid-afternoon when they neared the tiny town of Cliffside. Here Mr. Richards swung the faded blue station wagon and trailer, with its small motorboat, down the rutted, dusty road toward the cottage that would be their home for the next two weeks. Laboring under its heavy load, trailer bounced along between stately pines amid a pattern flecked in sun and shadow. Underneath branches of a huge Jack pine that stood near a red, weather-beaten, white-trimmed cottage, the station wagon sighed to a halt.

The last whir of the engine had hardly died when the car seemed to fall apart as the Richards family spewed forth. Tom was out in a twinkling; a twelve-year-old boy was much quicker than parents. His dad was the first to speak.

"It's good to be out of that sweatbox. Feel that ocean breeze."

Whispering through the branches of the great pine, the breeze did much to dispel the heat of a hot August day. For a moment they stood drinking in the sight and filling their lungs with the tantalizing aroma of salt and pine.

Mrs. Richards glanced at the cottage.

"Nothing's changed much," she said.

The camp had two small bedrooms, bath, kitchen nook, and a room that sufficed as a living and dining room. An unscreened porch slanted forward to near ground level. In the low-peaked structure was a loft where Tom slept. Entry was gained by a crude flight of stairs that were dropped from the ceiling by pulling a rope. A counterweight brought it back.

Two giant Jack pines bracketed the front, close by the cliff, where, some forty feet below, the ocean gently rolled. A path led along the cliff to Glencove a little over a hundred yards away.

Tom and his dad unloaded the station wagon while mother stacked foodstuffs in kitchen cupboards and busied herself with other necessary chores. Mr. Richards eventually joined her, and Tom, for the moment released from his task, seized the opportunity. Binoculars in hand, he hastily retreated through the swinging screen door that slapped shut behind him. Not hearing a call for assistance, he trotted to the Cliffside, wiped a sweaty right hand on blue jeans, brushed a wisp of blond hair from his eyes, and raised his binoculars to survey the great bay of the ocean. In the distance through the soft blue haze he could see the Stony Point Lighthouse at the north end of the bay. He swung the glasses to Harper's Island some three miles straight out and then looked at Gull Island close to the shore.

Finding little to hold his interest, he walked slowly toward the path that led to Glencove. His father's words echoed and re-echoed in his head – "I don't want you visiting old Ben Hardridge." But somehow his feet were taking him down the timeworn path to Ben Hardridge's cottage that sat on the bluff overlooking the boat landing.

As he came through the trees to the clearing where rays of late-afternoon sun bathed the tiny cottage, there was no sign of life outside, and no sounds emanated from within. For a time he gazed at the structure, then scanned the surrounding area. Curious, he pressed on to the edge of the bluff and looked down at the salt-stained boat house and weather-beaten plank dock. Nestled to the piling was the Wanderer, rising and falling on gentle swells that passed through one side of the cove and a natural ridge of rock that all but sealed the snug harbor. The gate to the ocean was about thirty feet across and took a little maneuvering in a high sea to navigate. He looked again at the ancient fishing boat with low cabin made for stowing equipment. The wheel just behind the cabin caught his eye. He smiled inwardly as he thought of fishing trips last summer and times Ben let him steer.

His spirits rose when he sighted Ben straddling the same paint-spattered, tool-scarred bench, bending to the task of fixing a lobster trap. Resistance failed him. He loped down the diagonal slanting path worn deep by generations of passing feet and on the dock to the old man's side.

"Hi Ben," he said.

Ben, his neck and back bent by the weight of work and years, peered out from under his burden.

"Hello, Tommy boy. I was wonderin' if I'd ever see ya' agin."

Hammer slipped from his grasp and a deeply tanned, gnarled hand reached out to tom. Tom clasped it warmly, gave it a few good shakes, which brought a gleam to gray eyes and a warm smile to his heavily lined face.

"Gonna stay a few weeks like ya did last summer?" Ben asked as he brushed back thin, snow-white hair.

"Yeah, Dad's only got a two-week vacation."

"Well, I cal'late I'll see 'im shortly, but you give 'im a hello for me when ya get back to camp."

Tom's smile disappeared quickly as he hesitated then said, "I'll do that."

Words of Wisdom

Ben leaned down, picked up a piece of lathe, and, grabbing his hammer, was about to start nails in each end of the slat. "If you'll allow, I'll work while we talk."

Tom shuffle uneasily but said nothing. Ben pounded the slat into place and, satisfied with the lobster trap, set it on the dock and slowly dragged a leg over the bench. Taking a few steps to a pile of traps near the boathouse, he selected one, placed it on the bench, and started to repair it.

"Gonna bring the boat down and do a little fishin'?"

"Guess we'll bring it down later this afternoon. I – I think I'd better get back to camp."

"Ya just got here, boy. We got a lot a talkin' to do."

"I know – but I've got to help straighten things out. I'll be back later."

"All right, son."

Tom turned and ran hurriedly from the dock and up the path. He burst through the screen door; the sound of its closing announced his arrival. His father, picking up an empty box, straightened his six-foot-two-inch frame and glared down at Tom.

"Where did you get to?"

Tom fidgeted, putting his weight on one foot then the other. His face warmed.

"I – I went down to the cove."

"By the way you look I know you were talkin' to Ben."

"Well he was on the dock and – "

"I don't care where he was. I told you not to see him and you deliberately went down there. I don't know what I'm going to do with you, Tom."

Tears filled the boy's eyes. With bowed head he moved to the rope connected to the loft stairs, brought them down, and retreated to his hideaway above. Mrs. Richards, standing solemnly to one side, addressed her husband. "Were you a little harsh, Ken? Maybe the old man does elaborate on the truth a little, but – "

"Lord in Heaven, you too, Ann? You know they're a pack of lies. Remember the one he told Tom about swimming six miles to shore in rough seas when the fishing boat he was on sunk off the coast? I'm going down there now and tell him to quit filling Tom's head with these tall stories."

"Ken, please don't go."

"I've got to put a stop to this once and for all."

Mr. Richards, jaw set, stalked out and headed down the path to the boat landing. Arriving at the bluff and sighting the old man still occupied with his task, he advanced on the hapless Ben. Ben heard him pounding down the dock and swiveled to see who was approaching.

"Mr. Richards, nice to see ya' agin."

Mr. Richards just nodded, face clouded as he said, "Ben, I don't want you to talk to Tom anymore. Those stories you've been filling his head with are nothing but lies."

"I never -- I never meant to hurt the boy, Mr. Richards. I just tell him things that happened to me in the past."

"Come now, you're not going to tell me all those things really happened."

"Well, you see, I -- "

Mr. Richards shook his head, snapped around, and departed, leaving Ben, mouth open, gesturing with his right hand.

Tom was still sulking the next morning over breakfast. Halfway through a bowl of cereal he looked at his mother, fussing over him more than usual.

"Mom, can I go down to the dock and fish awhile?"

"You'd better ask your father."

Tom looked at his dad, quite certain of the answer.

"Well, dad? Can I?"

"If you go down there you'll be talking to Ben and that's out."

Placing elbows on the table and burying head in hands Tom replied, "There's no one to play with and I can't even fish off the dock. What a rotten vacation this is goin' to be."

"Look, Tom, I don't want to hear any more about it. This afternoon we'll take the boat and do a little fishing."

Pushing the chair away from the table, Tom rose and, with head bowed, slowly shuffled out the front door.

At lunchtime, things were much the same. Tom disconsolately chewed on a peanut butter sandwich. His father glanced his way from time to time and finally addressed him. "As soon as we clean up after lunch, what say we catch some fish?"

"I don't want to."

"How about going out to Harper's Island? We can fish, scour the shore for shells, and maybe get some clams for supper."

"I'd rather stay here and find stones for my collection."

"I don't like to leave you here."

"I won't get into trouble. You and Mom go ahead. I'll be alright."

With lunch over and dishes put away, Tom's parents picked up the necessary fishing gear, and as they moved toward the dock his dad turned and gave Tom a parting shot.

"If you want to look for stones, try the creek that runs into the cove, but don't go near the beach."

Tom, head bowed, mumbled a half-hearted "Okay." He actually wanted to go to Harper's Island, where he could enjoy two of his favorite pastimes - fishing and searching for stones. He sat on the porch ledge, legs straight out into the path that trailed away to the landing, and rocked his feet back and forth, banging the toes of his fated white sneaks together. Thus he pondered his predicament, but only for a few minutes. His boundless energy could not be contained.

Rising, he turned to the back of camp, then angled off toward the stream. Reaching it, he headed downstream, taking little heed of leopard frogs that plopped into the cool waters of the meandering stream. Such things might have excited him, but not with mind preoccupied with thoughts of Ben. Even a blue heron rising majestically from a quiet pool did not disturb his thoughts. He knew, however, where the stream was taking him - to the cove and Ben. His father's shadow hung over it all like impending doom. Nevertheless, he moved slowly on, occasionally picking up a stone that caught his eye, until he arrived at a point close by the landing. Here he stood for a moment, heavy-hearted. Another bend and he would be in full view of the dock. His father's threats turned him from it. Scrambling up the bank, he trudged back to camp and, on arriving, went upstairs to place the newfound stones in his collection.

The sill of the loft window was little more than a foot above the floor. Here he often sat cross-legged, binoculars in hand, and from his vantage point surveyed the major part of the bay. As he fondled the bright stones, a sudden gust of wind rattled the windowpane. He took notice of a few drops of rain that pelted the glass, and then checked his wristwatch. It would be some time before his parents would return. Grasping his binoculars, he swept the outer limits of the bay. Dark water flecked with white caps mirrored an angry sky. Checking the small barren island where his parents had gone he found no sign of life. Lowering the glasses to see if they were on the way in, something caught his eye. Gull Island, or "the rock pile" as the natives called it, was a half-mile inside Harper's Island and here Tom's glasses picked up a white object.

As he steadied the binoculars and strained his eyes he could make out his father wearing a white sweatshirt and his mother, in light blue slacks and sweater, close beside him. They were standing on the one large flat rock still above the oncoming tide and battering waves of the storm's rising fury. There was no trace of the boat. As he watched, his dad waved arms violently. No doubting, they were in trouble.

Setting glasses aside, he scrambled from the loft, down the creaking stairs, through the screen door and across the yard. He sped down the path toward the cove.

"Ben is the only one nearby," he said to himself. "I must find him."

Sliding to a halt in front of Ben's cottage, he hopped to the stoop and pounded on the door. Ben was quick to coming. Looking at the boy's anxious face he inquired, "What's the matter, Tom?"

Tom, trying to catch his breath, blurted out, "Mom and Dad are on the rock pile. The waves are goin' right over it. Can you get them off?"

"We can try." He immediately set about gathering clothes and gear as if he had done it many times before.

"What happened to their boat?" Ben asked.

"I don't know. Saw them through my binoculars standin' on the large rock that's above the rest; couldn't see the boat anywhere."

Ben took a sideways glance at the front window that rattled from wind and hard driving rain.

"The way the rain's comin' down we couldn't see 'em either. I've got what I need, Tom. Let's get to the dock. Here, carry this hank of rope." He tossed it to Tom.

Out the door into the pelting rain they went. The wind no longer sighed in the pines, but roared its defiance, accompanied by booming surf on the cliff below. Hastily they retreated down the precarious slanting path to dock and Wanderer.

Concerned about his parents, Tom had left the cottage without raincoat or hat. Noticing the dripping head and wet t-shirt, Ben hurried to a tool shed and returned with poncho in hand. "Put this on boy, before ya' get the shakes." Tom pulled it over his head. Although large, it did shelter him from the slashing rain.

"Get ready to slip the bow line while I start the engine. I don't like to take you out but there's no one else around and I need your help.

"I want to go."

"I know ya do, but that's no place for a boy."

The old man was trying to stiffen his back for the voyage ahead, a voyage that would test him greatly.

The engine coughed to life. Ben looked at Tom. "Cast off and pick up that pike pole. We may need it as we sip through between piling and rocks to the bay."

Tom grasped the pole and stood straddle-legged near the bow, awaiting further developments. The old weather-beaten fishing boat swung slowly around the dock, hugging rocks that protected the cove from the heavy surf. Through the less turbulent water, Ben guided the craft until near the end of the barrier. Here he spun the wheel violently, skating the craft sideways, so that when it glided from its sanctuary, bow was directly into wind and wave.

The engine steadied to a regular beat. Creaking and groaning, the Wanderer crested the first wave, bow rising out of the water. It hung for a moment, dropped hard, and, with a great shaking, buried its nose deep into another wave, then labored to rise to the height, only to come shuddering down once more.

Doggedly, the old man held to wheel, head thrust forward, peering intently into the raging sea before him. Man, boy, and near-derelict boat fought slowly onward into the ever-increasing fury of the storm.

Tom looked at Ben and said, "I can't see a thing. Do ya think we can find 'em?"

"We'll find 'em boy, we'll find 'em."

Tom thought of his father's words: "He's nothing but a dreamer, boy."

Tom, now sitting with his back to the low cabin, looked at the timeworn, gnarled hands that tightly clasped the wheel.

"They sure don't look like a dreamer's hands," he said to himself.

Now the storm exploded with all its pent-up violence, arousing Tom from his thoughts. Wind howled over the gunwales and, with every wave, water joined it. The old boat didn't seem to have a chance, moaning in agony as each wave passed. Decks were awash. Ben hollered, "We're getting too low in the water. Get the bucket out of the cabin and bail like the devil."

On his knees in front of the cabin door, Tom disappeared inside, reappeared in a twinkling, and started to bail. Ben's eyes never dropped but stared straight ahead into the maelstrom. Wind-whipped spray licked from the breaking waves, joined its counterpart from the clouds above, and in sheets, lashed their faces unmercifully. Tears, rain, and salt water intermingled as they forged on.

"We're not makin' much headway," Tom shouted.

"Cal'late we'll get there soon, just keep that bucket goin'."

Tom wondered how he could find the rock pile that was Gull Island. Visibility was near zero. In his stomach was a sinking feeling as he thought of Mother and Dad clinging to that rock, in the terrible gale. Salt was heavy on his lips as he flung a bucket of water astern. A mountainous wave hammered the craft, almost knocking his legs from under him. Tom glanced at Ben. His red-checkered wool shirt clung to him like another skin. The rain gear he brought was still in the cabin.

"Don't you want that parka?" he hollered.

Over the roar of wind, wave, and the pop of the engine, came the reply.

"To hell with the parka, boy! I can't let go the wheel. Besides, it limits my action. How ya' comin' with the bailin'?"

"I'm holding my own. Do ya think we're anywhere near the rock pile?"

"Cal'late we're pretty close. Been followin' a track of suds made by the waves poundin' on Harper's Island. Wind curls it around the tip and it forms a line to the beach."

Tom didn't know exactly what he was talking about, but he hoped Ben was right. Maybe they were coming up behind the island. The waves didn't seem quite so high.

A half-mile inside and slightly toward the island's north end lay the rock pile. His mother and father would get little protection from the elements there. Minutes went by. The motor slowed. Tom stared at Ben.

"What's the matter?"

"I think I see somethin' off the port side."

Tom strained to see through the almost impenetrable curtain of rain ahead.

"There's somethin' there! I see a patch of white!"

"Can't turn broadside," shouted Ben. "We'll capsize! I'll sidle over; keep the bow into the waves."

They drew nearer. Tom could see the white object was his father, and then, against the blue-gray background, his mother close beside him. They were huddled together on bay side of the huge slanting rock, legs and arms bracing backs against cascading water that all but swept them from their perilous perch. Ben nosed the boat closer. Tom scurried forward and shouted, "Mom! Dad!" They looked in the direction of the voice. His dad was the first to answer.

"Good lord, son! How did you get here?"

Then, in the pounding surf, he noticed Ben close behind, manning the wheel.

"Tom!" Ben cried, "How far to the rock?"

"About ten feet."

"Mr. Richards, can ya hear me?"

"Yes."

"If the bow comes down on that rock, we're done. When I get near, grab the rail and throw yourself on deck. Then help Mrs. Richards on. Have ya got that?"

"Yes -- I'll try."

The Wanderer moved ever closer to the sharp edge of the rectangular rock, to which the near frantic Mr. Richards and his wife clung. Tom, with pike pole ready, sat near the bow. Crashing down, the Wanderer came within a foot of the rock; as it did so, Mr. Richards stood up, grasped the rail, and just before the bow rose, flung himself on deck. This accomplished, he steeled himself to pull his wife aboard. They drifted away. Mr. Richards knelt beside the rail and leaned forward, ready to grasp his wife's hand. Ben closed the gap and just before the bow rose on the crest of another wave, Mr. Richards lunged for her hand. As his hand tightened on hers he shouted, "Jump and hang on tight!"

She started, but her foot missed the bobbing deck and struck against the hull. She dropped, legs trailing in the water. Both hands held firm and Mr. Richards with great effort swung her aboard. For the moment they were safe.

The storm raged on with unabated fury. Ben let the craft ease away from the Richards' storm-lashed refuge. It afforded some protection and he swiveled the boat quickly without taking excess water. The engine throbbed with renewed vigor as if it knew it was heading home. Tom resumed bailing. Mr. Richards, half-standing, still grasping his wife's hand, helped her up and with a few halting stops, crossed the heaving deck and dropped back against the low cabin wall. Mr. Richard's arm encircled his wife's shoulders as he comforted her from the long ordeal not yet over. Less water was coming over the gunwales and Tom slowed down.

"Ben," he said, "We aren't takin' much water."

"That's good, but we've got to keep our speed up. We get caught in the wallow and slide back into the jaws of an oncomin' wave, it'll crash right over the transom and swallow us in one bite."

Tom gazed in amazement at the old man, fearing he would be done in by the strain. But he was as calm as if mending lobster traps back at the wharf. Over his right eye, however, was a slight cut. Tom figured he had banged it on the wheel in the rough seas. Reaching in his back pocket, he pulled to a clean white handkerchief and, although wet, placed it against the cut. The old man smiled.

"Thank ya boy. It'll be alright. "

His eyes were still fixed on the crashing sea that shook the frail craft mercilessly. Up and down towering waves they went, water licking the tops of gunwales and transom.

"Mr. Richards," Ben shouted, "Can ya go for'd and guide me in? Can't see a thing out there and I'm close to the beach."

Mr. Richards quickly obeyed, wondering how Ben knew. Tom's father was hardly situated on the bow when he cried out, "Rocks ahead!"

As the boat crested, Ben saw them too. He turned right, narrowly missing a huge boulder, then swerved left; the stern fish-tailed as a wave slapped it, nearly swinging bow against the massive barrier to their safety. Engine beat mounted, swinging the Wanderer back on course. It drove through the gap between rock and dock, piling to the safety of Glencove's quiet water.

Ben nestled the boat to the dock side, where a bedraggled, exhausted crew, still seeking shelter from shrieking wind and driving rain, struggled up the ladder and moved to the boathouse wall for protection. Mr. Richards grasped Ben's hand and pumped it vigorously.

"I don't know how to thank you. Still can't figure out how you found or got us back."

"Cal'late I've done it -- hundred times," said Ben. "That little frolic reminded me of the time I pulled Adam Howlett out of the water after his fishin' boat capsized."

Tom noticed his father's pained expression, followed by a slow shaking of head. Then his face softened into a broad smile as he placed a gentle hand on Tom's shoulder. Tom smiled too, a deep satisfying smile as he turned to gaze at his old and wonderful friend.

THE HIDEAWAY - WAY DOWN SKANEATELES LAKE

There is a place I go when the world closes in, just a small camp on the shore of Skaneateles Lake, a place to gain a little peace of mind, and it seems to come easier with a fishing rod in hand. I do not intend to convey the idea that I always catch fish and so arrive back at camp with a smile on my face. I could not care to say how many times my boat arrived without a full load or even one fish within its confines, but I do know that at times I disembark without fish and still somehow manage to smile.

It was early evening when I set out on the placid waters of the lake for a little relaxation and perhaps, if luck had not deserted me, an occasional lake trout might come my way. I gave a push with an oar to get the necessary depth to operate the little three-and-a-half horse motor, dropped it, gave a few pulls, and my small boat cut the mirrored waters. Chugging to a spot, some 150 yards off camp, I turned north paralleling the shore and throttled down to trolling speed.

I picked up my battered old pole, snatched the spoon from its position where it clung to the reel and tossed it into the dark green waters. I pushed the button releasing the drag, thumbed the reel lightly, and the thread-like wire peeled off rapidly. Now the spoon some 80 feet below the surface was wig-wagging along, flirting with the lake trout a scant foot off bottom. I started the pumping rhythm swinging the pole forward then dropping back; this being accepted procedure when trolling for lake trout in Skaneateles. I always feel a lake trout will strike a soon as I get the lure down but that is rarely the case.

My attention to business soon waned, as the finny monsters in the depths did not care to communicate. I turned my attention elsewhere, feasting my eyes on the nearby hill that rose behind camp to a height bordering a thousand feet. Solid timber, a sea of light and dark green; maples, oak and hemlock grew there in gay profusion, the beauty of that sheer wall was appreciated by the simple fisherman like me. I was jolted from my appraisal of the scene by some interloper on the far end of the line. Halfway through the pickup of the wire, my pole stopped short, bent, then throbbed as a head-shaking laker tried to get rid of a hard tasteless piece of hardware. The lure held fast and after holding bottom for a time, the steady pressure began to tell and the fish slowly started the ascent to the boat. After some thrashing on the surface, the trout came to the waiting net. I placed the colorful fish on a stringer and again dropped the spoon overboard. The ritual was repeated twice more. Now I had my limit of three lakers and so, smiling inwardly, I turned the boat campward.

I had been on the lake less than two hours and so could not complain about the fishing. It was nice to know that fish could still be caught in my own backyard. The day left little to be desired. I would not have designed a better one. As I straightened from my hunched position, over my tackle, I looked at the dark brooding hills on my right that were casting shadows on their counterparts across the lake

I drank in the tranquil scene and it brought me greater satisfaction.

Edwin Lukens

THE LAST MILE

The spell of the Garden was upon him. He stood looking at the wooden saucer and through his mind's eye, marched races out of the past. Memories flooded his head, of battles won and lost in better days when many a mile race was run and the name of Tom Hill meant something.

Tom was tall, sandy-haired, and slender of frame Not an ounce of fat on him – there never had been. He had sharp features with a slight distortion, this being a bent nose garnered long ago on another field of endeavor. His intense gray eyes mirrored 18 years of dedication to track.

Several years had gone by since he last trod these boards, pock-marked by many a spiked foot. With military service and a long conditioning period, five years had slipped by. Perhaps he was living on false hopes. Many an athlete thought he could return to past glories, only to fall flat on his face. He was simply a "has-been" returning to the battleground of old with little hope of success. In greener years there was more spring in his legs. This thought bothered him. Actually, his only hope rested in his ability to run a faster pace and take the kick out of the others. Wilson, the best of the group, would more than likely set an early pace. He hoped he could hang on.

There were so many "ifs" tied to the race. One thing was certain: the rest of the field had little fear of him. If he kept near the front end or even took the lead, no one would give it a second thought, figuring he would never last. As far as they were concerned, he was "over the hill."

Tom walked to the dressing room. The smell of liniment was everywhere. The odor of oil of wintergreen came to him. It was like the most fragrant perfume. Seating himself on one of his old dilapidated benches between the lockers, he proceeded to prepare for the biggest race of his life.

There was only one man in the field he had ever met before. Martin was a youngster then, now a seasoned veteran. He glanced up the alley to where Martin was sitting. Martin saw him, nodded, and shortly moved toward him. They exchanged pleasantries, shook hands, and, seating himself, Martin said, "It's been a long time."

"Yes," Tom answered, "a long time. Maybe too long. But it's good to be back again if only for one race." A wisp of smile twisted his lips.

Martin shook his head and gave him a knowing look. "An athlete's career can be pretty short...too short," he said.

Tom knew Martin was thinking of him when he said it, and he appreciated the concern he saw in Martin's face.

"You know," he said to Martin, "I've been working over a year for this race and have averaged over eighty miles a week. To put it bluntly, it's been some grind. I've had to sacrifice many things, but it would all be worthwhile for one more smell of the roses."

"You know these guys better than I. I'm sure the whole field – Wilson, Jansen, Boyce, Conti, and yourself included, can outkick me. What do you think the pattern will be?"

"On the record, Wilson is the best man. He can outkick us all and will probably take the lead at the outset to make some of them run a bit. Then a few of the boys may slide by if they figure they have enough left. Wilson will dog them playing cat and mouse, then with a lap or two to go, he'll take off. The only way you can get him is to take the kick out of him with a faster pace and that's difficult to do."

Tom said, "Well, we can try." Quickly, he added, "I'm lucky to be here at all. They only let me in the race because of courtesy for past performances and possibly a need to fill up the field."

Just then Elmer Garrow, sportswriter for the Monitor, swung around the lockers and made straight for Tom. They had met many times before and Tom cared little for his methods of constantly prodding men to the point of argument in order to get a spicy story. Tom was ready for him. With a wry, all-knowing smile, as if he was certain of the answers to his questions, he addressed Tom.

"Hasn't it been the better part of five years since you've run in competition?"

"Yeah, it's been about five."

"Do you think you have a chance?"

Tom stared at Garrow for a moment. "I'm just running for laughs," he said.

Garrow smiled, turned away, and muttered as he shuffled out, "That may be all you'll get."

Tom thought differently, however. He had tasted sweet victory and bitter defeat, but any man who showed up to lose didn't belong in any race.

Tom finished dressing, rose, and with Martin following, slowly headed toward the arena to prepare for the race. As he entered, a shiver went through him. Once again, he would feel the Garden boards under his feet, hear the drumming of the pack as they jockeyed for position, and the rising roar of the crowd as the competitors vied for the lead.

The nerves were jangling a bit now as he warmed up. He jogged, did calisthenics, strode awhile, and then breathed deeply as he awaited the start. He was prepared as could be for the battle to come. Sweats were peeled off and somewhat hesitantly the contestants sauntered to the starting line. They shook hands, then stepped to their assigned places.

The nervous movements stopped as they froze on command. Six men moved off in unison as the gun roared. Wilson had the pole on the first turn. Martin and Jansen followed close behind with Tom tucking into fourth position; Boyce and Conti brought up the rear. Around and around the saucer they went, still closely packed in and in the same order as they swept past the quarter mark. Tom, knowing his only hope was a faster pace, edged around Jansen and Martin, challenged Wilson, lock stepping for half a lap before he took the lead. Wilson was, no doubt, smiling inwardly, figuring Tom would never last, just take the lead awhile, then fade out of the picture. At the half-mile mark, Tom caught the time – two minutes, four seconds. It wasn't fast enough. He'd have to pick up the pace. With a quarter to go, eight yards separated Tom and Wilson.

At this point, Martin and Jansen jockeyed by Wilson and settled in. Perhaps they figured Wilson wasn't on his race and Tom, who was getting too far out, might last. Tom's lead had stretched to twelve yards. He heard the chant, two laps to go. Now the whole pack was starting to close the gap. On guts alone, doggedly Tom held on. Over and over he called on his old legs to move. "It's now or never," he thought. "The whole race is in my grasp." The gun roared in his ear. One more lap, just one more. "Lord help me." He hadn't died yet, but the time was close at hand.

A scant four yards back, Jansen on the pole and Martin trying to pass, were side by side. Wilson, two yards behind them, was making his bid, and as he hit the first turn, he pulled slightly ahead of the two men who blocked his path. Not getting the necessary lead to cut in, he was forced to run high up the banked turn, losing valuable yards. Jansen and Martin, still stride for stride, came off slightly ahead and still had him boxed. Tom's mind was calling for a kick, but the body could not answer.

On painful, rubbery legs he struggled on, a stride ahead of the three men fighting to wrest his race from him. Into the last turn came Wilson, summoning all the drive at his command. He slipped by the tandem in front and closed in on Tom. Above the cheers of the frenzied throng, Tom could hear him pounding at his back and called on one last gasp of nervous energy to see him home. Through glassy eyes the boards were jumping about and although the tape beckoned, he could not see it. Wilson came relentlessly on, just a few feet away, as Tom's legs started to buckle. He pitched forward. His agony was also his moment of glory, for headlong through the tape he went, inches ahead of Wilson.

Crashing to the boards, picking up splinters, he slid, then rolled, to a stop. Two officials helped him up as he tried desperately to get his legs under him. The crowd, who had taken the old man to heart, shouted their approval. Somehow through the din he understood. Victory was his. With assistance he received his medal to the plaudits of the multitude and flashing cameras. Still gasping for breath, he tottered to the dressing room. Sitting on the rickety bench, back against the lockers, he fondled his medal. They could take this away and he wouldn't care, but the race was his and could never be taken away from him.

The long lonely hours spent grinding out the miles, preparing for this race, had paid off. Martin sat down beside him. Tom spoke.

"I heard you and Jensen had Wilson boxed. I know you were running for yourself; nevertheless, you may well had saved my bacon."

"I don't know about that, you ran a tremendous race. I don't mind saying you surprised the devil out of me, even if I did know the training you'd been through. "

Garrow had come into the locker room a few moments before. Wedging through the ring of athletes and sportswriters, he stood listening to the conversation. Moving closer, he stared coldly down at Tom, who was accepting congratulations and answering questions. His face softened with a warm smile.

"Just running for laughs, huh?"

Looking up, Tom forced a weary smile but said nothing.

Garrow went on, "I thought you were a lost cause, old man, and I think everybody else did. I guess you were the only one that believed otherwise." Hesitating a moment, he added, "I suppose you'll run the rest of the indoor season."

"No...I'll never run in competitions again."

"After that race?"

"I only wanted to run once more, just to prove that I could come back. That was my last mile."

"Sorry to hear that. You ran one of the greatest races I ever saw."

Tom thanked him. Garrow wished him luck, turned, and walked out.

The race had taken its toll. It would be several days before he could walk, let along run, without pain. The room had cleared but for Martin, still seated beside Tom. He showered, dressed, and with Martin at his side, moved with some effort toward the door.

Martin spoke. "How ya doin', old man?"

"Pretty good, youngster. Legs are cramped and a little shaky, but I can struggle out of here."

They passed through the dressing room doors and out into the corridor. Coming to one of the aisles that led to the arena, Tom excused himself for a moment. He shuffled in and stood gazing at the tiers of empty seats. A short time ago the crowd roared with his every stride; now, it was haunted. Well he thought, at least I left them a race to remember.

As if addressing the Garden, he said to himself with a twinge of sadness, "That's my last race, old friend. You'll see me no more."

Slowly, on stiff, aching legs, Tom struggled out, turning his back on the Garden forever.

THEY CALL IT ICE FISHING

It was my belief that duck hunters were the craziest breed of sportsmen alive; that is, until I was introduced to the brotherhood of ice fishermen. In weather too cold for polar bears, thy sit or stand like statues, peering into a hole, with all the intensity of a rube watching his first burlesque show. From the warmth of cars and homes, unbelievers shake their heads at the sight of little knots of men huddled together on the ice. Men looking more like prehistoric monsters, backs into the wind and swirling snow, with mackinaw collars high and heads drawn in like turtles.

Many a member of this zany band has come up against a problem or two. The wife of one buff threatened to leave him unless he broke the habit. He went to a psychiatrist in search of a cure. The doctor asked several questions including one about his prowess as a fisherman. He told him about the limit catches of walleye he had been getting. After a few more couch visits the doctor said, "I think you're cured, but if you have a relapse pick me up."

When you mix with the strange breed, strange things happen. One morning as I ventured out on the ice I came upon two members of the fraternity fishing with minnows. After asking them how they were doing, I continued to chat for a while. Distracting them from their task, one of the bobbers went down unnoticed. By the time they spotted it, most of the slack line coiled on the ice was gone. One of them made a run for it at the same time his partner noticed the bobber dancing on his own line. The resulting action was something to behold. Both men tugged furiously, thinking they had hooked the biggest fish in the lake. The tug of war went on for some time until it finally dawned on them that the fish had swallowed both minnows. Rather sheepishly, one released the line and let the other pull a small hungry walleye through the hole.

My ice fishing knowledge and enjoyment was enhanced to some degree after I met Charley.

Charley is a veteran ice fisherman who says, "The only good thing about ice fishing is the fact ya can't get inta' hot water." Of course that depends on how you look at it. Once I asked Charley what it takes to be an ice fisherman. His reply was typical: "To be an ice fisherman, ya need two holes, one in the ice an' the other in your head."

Old Charley's exploits deserve some telling. Once he ventured forth on some early December ice that didn't bear up under the strain. After splashing around awhile, he finally bellied his way to good ice and made it to shore. A few days later I asked him how he enjoyed his swim. He said it was so cold he didn't feel it 'till the next day.

On one of my excursions with my old friend, two fellows stopped close by and, after spudding in a few holes, immediately started jigging. Jack perch were popping out of the holes with great rapidity so Charley wandered over to see what they were using to entice the fish. While there I heard him say, "Ya better make them holes a little bigger, there's northern around here ya know." "I don't think we'll run into any," came the reply. Charley shrugged his shoulders and returned to his fishing.

About a half-hour later, things began to happen over at the neighbor's place. It seems there was a big northern on one of the lines and they couldn't get him through the hole. One guy was holding the line while the other chopped like mad. Even Charley's glass eye was aglow as he jumped up and down roaring with laughter. When his convulsions ceased he turned to me and said, "Did ya ever see a guy spud so fast, looked like he was on a hand car with a locomotive on his tail?"

I remember one time when Charley was wounded in combat. He had just finished draining a bottle of wine when a fish struck his jig rig. In his haste he fell off the minnow bucket he was sitting on and broke his nose. This was the only physical damage he ever received but he suffered many a mental shock. Most notable was the time he took three of us fishing. Yes, Charley could drive very well with his one good eye. When we arrived at our destination we found many fishermen driving on the ice. Although Charley loved his light blue Ford, he figured it was safe enough and it would save us a long walk.

In a few minutes we were there. Charley had just acquired a new auger that he enjoyed using very much, so he immediately started boring holes with reckless abandon. About an hour later the fishing had tapered off. Charley decided to put in a few more holes. He was drilling away close by the car when the ice cracked and streaks raced back and forth between holes. It gave way, ice cake tipped up and thumped underneath the vehicle. Then the car slid backward. Water splashed around and eventually over the top, as Charley's light blue Ford settled slowly to the bottom, some twenty feet below. In the dark water ice cakes bobbed and thousands of bubbles came streaming up. Charley's mouth was wide open as he peered into the hole with his one good eye. But Charley recovered quickly. There was a wisp of a smile on his lips as he looked at me and said, "I don't think we'll catch much with it, baits a mite big for anythin' in this pond." I didn't argue the point.

The car still rests in its watery grave. However, it wasn't a total loss. Bass seem to like the light blue Fords. In the summertime the fishing's great around it. Oh yes, Charley bought another car and he drives it on the ice. We often chide him about the color. You see, it's two-tone, brown and yellow, and we can't wait to see it drop through and find out what kind of fish it attracts.

Edwin Lukens

TO SURVIVE

Between rocky tag alder-sprinkled banks, crowned with spruce, flowed a mighty river northward to the sea. From the thin line of spruce brooding monuments of rock rose, their tops curtained by a blanket of clouds.

A foreign buzzing sound came into the valley, silenced the leaves of tag alders gentled by a wisp of river breeze. The faint buzzing mounted, became a drone, shutting out the White Crowned Sparrow's song, and then the staccato drowned all sound that emanated from the valley.

Around a mountain of rock, scarcely one hundred feet above the water, bored a Beaver floatplane. Northward it flew, with river's flow, but the destination was a hundred and sixty miles east.

Alone, Brad Owens rode the sky. He hunched forward, peered at the right wall, hoping for a break in overcast clouds that would unlock a saddle and allow him to slip through – to no avail. With little more than enough gas to see him home, he prepared to dump and wait it out. The river ahead being wide and seemingly without obstacles, he wheeled the Beaver and scanned the water below once more. Satisfied, he leveled off, throttled down, and dropped the plane in a shower of spray. Cutting current, he angled for the east bank, but close in the left pontoon struck a submerged rock whipping the plane away. Now crosswise with the river's flow, it drifted swiftly toward menacing rapids a half mile below. Battling fast water and breeze, Brad fought the plane around and headed for the bank again. Lost were three hundred yards to the ever-increasing current.

The river shallowed where it narrowed down to the pitch at rapid's mouth. A picket fence of rock denied him the bank. He hit the throttle hard to pull out and up river to quiet water away from danger. Tacking against river's thrust, pontoons ran deep, plowing water and then, for the second and last time, it happened. The middle of the right float smashed hard into rock hiding just below the surface. The plane shuddered violently and Brad heard a snapping sound as he bucked forward over the controls. He feared the worst and the worst was with him. The undercarriage had sheared off and the right pontoon was now free. Leaving no support, the right wing dropped into the water, swept deep as the left float grated along the rock then moved away. The fuselage began to fill. Brad slammed the door open, hoisted himself out, and, as the plane settled low, jumped and thrashed for shore.

Sub-Arctic temperatures had kept the water ice cold and the shock of it took air from his lungs and made him fight to get it back. A boulder loomed. He started to sweep by, lunged, got a handhold, and pulled himself up. His eyes were transfixed on the plane as it dropped over the pitch into the jaws of the deadly rapids and disappeared below. It was as if he had lost his only friend. Sadly turning away, eyeing another boulder closer in, Brad gauged the current for a moment, and then slid off his tiny sanctuary. Passing above his goal, he instinctively made for firm ground. Nearing exhaustion, he clawed at the steep rock-strewn shoreline and collapsed on a mossy bank where he lay for some time.

The water's penetrating cold had bored into the very core of life itself. With convulsive effort he roused himself to gather driftwood left by spring breakup. Satisfied that he had the makings of a good fire, the wood was deposited in lee of a huge boulder. Fingers stiffened from the cold made it difficult to unbutton the pocket of his wool shirt. He tore at the flaps, ripping the button off, and plucked a match case from the pocket. He proceeded to start the kindling. A roaring fire ensued. Grudgingly, deep cold gave way to fire's warmth.

As life rose anew he collected his thoughts. All he had were the clothes on his back, a penknife, the waterproof case of matches, and a bottle of insect repellent. Emergency rations were on the plane. The base was one hundred and sixty miles away. The land between, slashed by river valleys, lakes, mountains, and muskeg would be an impossible journey. His location was not known as the walls of the valley and heavy Borealis activity had denied communication with the base. Thoughts switched to the nearest point of civilization – an out camp prospecting crew some forty miles down river.

Destination decided upon, he arose, snuffed the fire, and started the trek, not wanting to waste the six hours of daylight that remained. Laboriously, he walked the rocky shore that punished his ankles severely, glancing from time to time at the raging rapids, hoping to sight the plane, but it was not to be.

A mile gained, he stopped, tucked a wisp of brown hair under his red leather cap and bemoaned the extra weight that made him breathe so heavily.

The march continued through the long afternoon and evening until, finally, he prepared for night. Hungry, but not severely, he searched for blueberries. Finding none, the river was checked, although he did not know how the catching of fish could be accomplished without any gear. The shallows held nothing, so he built a fire beneath a rock overhang and settled down. Several miles had been covered but under the toil of the tortuous trail he wondered how long he could endure. For the first time he was alone, in the cold, and the dark. He cursed his predicament in the wilderness. A wilderness that he held little in common with in the past would now control his destiny.

The chill of night upon him he fed the fire and leaned back against a solid face of rock. The wind made sleep spasmodic; one side was warmed by the flickering flames while the other nearly froze.

Dawn's first light was welcome, although legs lamed by cold and exertion were slow to respond, and hunger pains were hard on him. Not long on the trail, he came upon a small patch of blueberries and gleaned a few handfuls, which allayed his hunger and lifted his spirits.

For the first time, the sun broke through the overcast clouds. Its warmth was welcome but it brought forth a determined horde of black flies that tormented him, and when a blind bay fringed with tag alders was reached, mosquitoes set upon him in clouds, and, but for insect repellent, would have driven him into a frenzy.

The sun was still high in the heavens but his legs, cramped and pained, would no longer do his bidding. In a saddle carpeted with Caribou Moss, he rested.

Eventually, in stages, he came erect and haltingly surveyed the small crystal clear stream close by. To his amazement, he found graveled pockets alive with brook trout. Anticipation overwhelmed him and yet, not knowing how to extract the treasure, he sat and pondered the problem. Finally he decided upon a simple scheme: try to hit them with rocks. One was lifted and cast, tearing a hole in the shallow pool at his feet. When the spray, bubbles, and sediment cleared, not one dead fish could be seen. Dejected, he tried again. In the aftermath, one trout nearly a foot long rose to the surface and slowly floated belly-up at the base of the pool. Brad splashed in, stuck his fingers in the fish's gills, then brought his prize shoreward and tossed it on the ground.

Returning to the task, he was, in time, rewarded once more. Drained by exertion but elated, he set about to prepare his life-giving meal. The fish was placed on sticks that were anchored and angled over the fire, making cooking easier. Ravenously, he fell upon them and soon consumed all. Hunger pains subsided to some extent; he lay back on the Labrador bank and contemplated for the moment, brighter hopes for survival.

Daylight died but this night found him more at peace with his surroundings. Without wind, the fire's range widened. Its added warmth and a spruce bough bed helped alleviate aching muscles and soon he slept the deep sleep of wanderers of the wilderness.

In early light he rose to greet a day that hopefully would see him much closer to his goal. Fishing in the same fashion without success, he turned to the trail. Even though his legs were hobbled, many miles lay behind when he made camp. Failing to find anything to eat in the immediate area, disconsolately he curled up before the fire and, as undulating waves of northern lights rolled across the heavens, he slept.

Hunger gnawed deep in his innards when he awoke and continued the journey toward a distant destination, a destination that had to be reached if he were to live. More pressing was the immediate problem – to sustain life. The rugged terrain and cold were taking their toll. As he trudged along hoping to find more fish, he blundered on a

Ptarmigan. It flew a short distance and landed in a small Tamarack. Finding a stick he stalked the bird, but just as the club was about to descend, protesting legs caused him to stumble. The bird flushed and disappeared over a high bank. Disgusted, he slumped down to regain strength.

Near midday, he came upon a small inlet. In the confines of a shallow sandy-bottomed pool was a school of minnows. But for a thin channel they were cut off from the river. Brad, hastening to close the gap with rocks, tottered and fell headlong into the pool. Some of the minnows escaped in the confusion; however, most remained.

The job done, he cut a thin pole and began to flail the water, hoping it would stun the fish. After striking several times he watched intently, then eagerly collected a few minnows that floated up and deposited them on shore. Several times the process was repeated until no more fish could be found. Skewered on a stick and toasted over the fire, the meager meal was quickly cooked and devoured. He rested, thankful for food and the warmth of fire, and then moved on.

By day's end, good progress had been made and with some satisfaction he bedded down. A few hours later he stirred to the lick of a determined upriver wind on his cheek. Spawned in the Arctic Ocean, it would, in short order, cause the temperature to plummet twenty degrees or more. He fed the fire and repeated the process twice more before daybreak.

The ever-mounting wind, strong from the north, had a winter's edge. He had been blessed by southern flow, the only wind to bring any semblance of warmth to this sub-arctic land. Now he would fight weather that could easily bring snow. Buffeted by the cruel wind that pierced flimsy clothing, his feeble movements could not fight off the penetrating cold. He was impelled to swing into a draw that creased the riverbank. A fire was made, and when the chill had been driven out he pressed on. Much greater was the need for food.

Throughout the long afternoon and early evening, he stopped to warm himself repeatedly and still covered several miles. Twilight found him making camp in a cleft of face rock. He clambered over bordering, sloping masses of rock to collect boughs to lie upon from scraggly Spruce above. Returning down the smooth slope, little understanding nature's pitfalls, no heed was paid to her warning. On the rock was a tracing, stained and wet, where water seeped down from the ground above. Warmed occasionally by the sun, algae grew, making it extremely slippery. Brad stepped on the tracing, fell heavily, and slid toward the boulder-strewn shoreline below. His right leg wedged between two larger rocks, pitching him violently forward. He heard the snap and felt the stabbing pain that followed. Eyes blurred, he started to lose consciousness, but held on. Trying to straighten his body, the pain was nearly unbearable and nausea descended.

Now above the trapped leg, he eased it out. Although badly misshapen below the knee, no bone protruded from it. Stripping some of the spruce boughs that had dropped nearby, taking belt and handkerchief, he cradled the broken leg between two rocks and, hooking his heel, agonized it straight. Hoping it would set right, he tied splints and then slowly backed toward the campsite a stone's throw away.

He labored many minutes to gain his goal. He stared at the spot where the accident had occurred, hardly believing the time expended. Dark thoughts traversed his brain; they all but consumed his being. Now that he was crippled how could he escape this harsh and barren land? He wondered about the distance to the prospecting camp. Was it ten miles, twenty, or more? What did it matter – a broken leg, brutal terrain, might as well be one hundred. A fitful sleep was his that night, the dark hours occupied with throbbing leg and troubled mind.

At dawn he dragged himself to some driftwood. Finding bleached, tough pieces of spruce that fitted the purpose, he trimmed, tested the makeshift crutches, and then started to hobble downriver. It was a deadly game; traveling through rocks far thicker than monuments in a graveyard afforded little opportunity to swing crutches. An hour passed with just a few hundred yards gain. He dropped the crude instruments and lay on the riverbank. Like an ominous harbinger of death, an Osprey circled overhead. Exhausted, hungry, cold, and near panic, he faced the bleak future. All the forces of nature seemed aligned against him.

Finally, as if in a trance, he struggled up and set out. The broken leg not only denied movement, but food. To escape starvation he would have to find more berries and fish. His feeble efforts were ponderously slow and severely limited. Near collapse, he rested – the eternal thought burning deep inside: how to get out? Time after time he came up empty. Eventually it struck him. Heart beating strongly, hopes rose with the answer – a raft. The timeless river flowing strong through a thousand years would see him home to his destination and salvation.

To drag poles of size to water's edge would be difficult and timber on the fringe of the Barrens was scarce. Moving on, looking for a few windfalls to start the raft, he came upon a promontory of rock projecting well out into the river. By breaking current it created a giant black eddy. In spring floods, it caught the refuse of the might river and as water receded it was left high and dry.

Weak from lack of food, he paused frequently. It was a tedious task, pulling often from a sitting position, then dragging himself or using crutches for a few feet only to continue the process.

As the day wore on, materials were assembled. Thin springy poles for cross pieces were notched and placed near the ends toward the bottom of the raft where they would be used to clamp larger poles. Taking the leather thongs from boots, he cut lengths to hold the thin-notched poles in position. His last vestige of hope finished, he tested the raft and found it seaworthy. Two poles were selected for locomotion. As long as he could set pole to bottom he thought himself safe. Little daylight and strength remained when he ventured forth, not only to gain ground, but also to find a small inlet where fish might be confined.

For a time, the river ran in a glassy glide that propelled the raft without mishap. Bordering on delirium he laid back, not heeding the draw of the river. When he roused from his reverie, strong in his ear was the voice of great rapids. Struggling to his knees, he grabbed a pole and tried to check the raft's gathering speed, but with the river's pull and his weakened condition, it was impossible. Now he belonged to the river. He gazed in awe as the raft swept over the pitch. Below the hump of smooth water, huge rocks raked the raging river to shreds. Beyond, it funneled into a rock-walled gorge where there were no exceptions. It became a seething cauldron of white water, a river gone mad. He thought, "Nothing can survive in that maelstrom, not even fish." He dropped on his stomach with a death grip on the poles.

Plunging on, the frail craft shot between massive boulders and into the chute of white water. The raft was swallowed in surging froth and foam but by some miracle emerged unscathed to circle quietly on the back eddy of the placid pool below. Without movement he laid, cold, wet, suffering from exposure, the flame of life ebbing low. He strained to turn on his side and view the near shore. He thought, "I conquered the rapids but death is close at hand."

As the raft swirled slowly back toward the base of the great rapids, a light-colored object caught his eye. He lifted his head, and in the fading light blinked to chase away the ghostly shadows from his eyes. Hypnotized, he stared in disbelief.

"It's a tent," he said to himself, and then saw two more close by. He called out; a croaking sound escaped his lips but died, masked by the rapids' roar. The raft started to swing away from shore and out toward the thrust of the river, the river that would now sweep him past the prospecting camp to oblivion. Too weak to pole, hope for salvation fading fast, he glanced at the nearest tent, only a hundred yards away. He saw the camp cook, in white apron, step from the tent with bucket in hand and head for the river. Once again he called, to no avail. He raised an arm and the cook, idly appraising the expanse of water, stopped short, but the low raft and prone cargo did not register. Brad, summoning all the strength at his command, gained a sitting position. Through misty eyes he saw the cook drop the pail and run toward a beached canoe.

The battle with the wilderness was over. He had endured.

WELL-REMEMBERED

He was three years old when they moved to the house that would be the family homestead for 53 years. Father wanted Tim and his older brother to grow up near the edge of town, where open country beckoned. The house was on the fringe of a section of town known as "Skunk City." A short walk up a steep hill lay the Woodland Reservoir. A half mile away a park and still farther a farm with woodland and gully where flowed a crystal clear laughing stream.

At an early age he took his father's hand on summer evenings and they would climb the hill to play catch or just enjoy the countryside. When he did not make a clean catch or fell in his play, a little squeeze and shake of his father's hand on the nape of his neck made his world seem right again.

Tim remembered the Sunday afternoon picnics in a favorite spot by a waterfall where a large, flat rock served as a table. He waded in the cool stream water. Father pointed out the fascinating live things. "Look at the water spiders," and, lifting a rock, "Here's a crayfish." He poked a stick in front of it and Tim delighted as it darted backwards to safer haunts. They watched the Chubb minnows and occasionally sighted the wary brook trout as it flashed from open pool to sanctuary beneath undercut bank. Together they walked the glen many times, Tim's father imparting knowledge of flora and fauna…trillium, hepatica, adders tongue…oriole, cardinal, and song sparrow. With the changing seasons, father and son viewed skeins of Canadian honkers crossing autumn sky and with winter on the land, tracks of rabbit, pheasant, and fox.

The years moved relentlessly on but the knowledge imparted by his father of woodland and athletic field held him. There were fishing trips with his dad; walks to stream and pond for trout and perch; and, when they were successful, tasty morsels for the table.

Tim pitched for the neighborhood team. It was just a sandlot affair. The games were usually played on Saturday mornings at the nearby park. Often his father watched, emotionally charged, with the ebb and flow of the contests.

There was a beautiful day in late May when the high school track teams in the area met in a championship meet. The first call for the high hurdles was announced. Tim kept warming up. When the second call was made he reported to the clerk, stretched a bit, checked the blocks and ran through a few hurdles. Now he was ready.

He heard the starter's command: "On your marks."

He crouched in the blocks.

"Set," the starter said.

Gun roared and six contestants in unison drove toward the first barrier. At the fourth hurdle he was in the lead and at the sixth, nearly a stride ahead. He bore down on the seventh and in haste dropped his leg too soon. Heel smashed into top rung driving it forward. Knee of trail leg caught the dancing hurdle and he sprawled full length on the cinder track. He knew the race was over but he struggled up and finished. When the last event was run and the score tabulated, Tim's team had placed second, losing by two points. To Tim, the beautiful day was bathed in shadow, for he carried the weight of the loss. Disconsolately he trudged to the locker room and, after showering, moved toward the stadium gate where his father was waiting.

"I sure messed the meet up," he said to his father.

"There will be meets on other days," his father answered. "This one will serve as a stepping stone. You'll be a better athlete and a better man in years to come."

He felt the electricity of his father's hand as it came to rest on the nape of his neck and shook him. . . .

Tim entered the room. The nurse said, "It won't be long."

He looked down at the gray-haired, sunken-cheeked old man. He reached down, placed a hand on his father's shoulder, and squeezed it lightly. For a moment the misty green eyes opened; a wisp of a smile crossed the gaunt face.

He understood.

Edwin Lukens

WHAT GOES UP MUST COME DOWN – SOMEWHERE

The gas drum was dropped from the Otter float plane into the water, towed ashore, and rolled up the beach. Some cans of stove oil and other supplies were unloaded and packed away. With two days respite before guiding the next fishing party, Jim and I would fly back to the base with Brad Drake, the pilot, and get de-bushed, as guides and prospectors in the Canadian wilderness refer to it.

After several weeks in the bush, 130 miles west of the Labrador border town of Schefferville, we would welcome the respite. Brad standing on the float hollered, "Let's get goin'."

"What's the hurry?" I said as I picked my way out on the floating spruce dock that hardly kept me above water.

Brad replied, "I'm gonna swing a bit northeast and see what that prospecting outfit that abandoned camp on Larch Lake left behind."

Jim broke in. "We haven't much time before nightfall."

"If we don't run into a little weather, we'll make it," Brad said.

He taxied the Otter slowly out into the river, headed into the wind and wave and gunned the engine. With the light load, it jumped off the water. Brad swung the plane from river across spruce, tamarack, and caribou moss and before him to the horizon a myriad of lakes and roaring crystal clear rivers whose waters would soon mingle with the outer reaches of the Arctic Ocean.

Jim changed the subject. "Let's get movin' – those clouds are getting' darker."

"Okay," Brad answered, "We can use those plywood tent decks and sides back at the base and for the new tent camp and Trout Lake. We'll load it as far forward as we can."

The plywood, shovels, picks, fire extinguishers, ash cans full of quart containers of oil and a few other things were loaded as well. We finished the task but lightning was cracking off to the west and closing in to the south, our direction of flight.

Brad surveyed the situation and said, "We'd better hole up for a spell."

The cook shack being a more permanent structure seemed like a good spot. Bears had smashed the door in, but the rest of the building was intact. Shelves had been loaded with foodstuffs. Now most were scattered and smashed. Cans were shredded by tooth and claw; jars of jelly and strawberry preserves were broken.

Jim said, "I imagine the bears loved the preserves but I wonder how much glass went down too. That would be a little problem."

The storm fell in full fury and lasted for some time. Night would soon be upon us and thoughts of staying here crossed our minds.

Brad spoke, "Clouds seem to be lifting. It looks pretty good to the south. Let's hold a few more minutes and then if there's an opening, we'll make a run for it."

Jim said, "You'll be landing in the dark, Brad."

Brad replied, "What bothers me most is checking map and terrain so that we find the base."

His eyes searched the sky. "Get aboard. We'll move out and get ready for takeoff."

Brad climbed to the pilot's seat. Jim and I unfastened ropes and placed them in the tail compartment.

"Brad," I hollered. "We've got an awful load on this plane. A third of the floats are under water."

"We're okay," he replied, "most of the weight's up front and there's a lot of lake to make a run on." I was secretly hoping he was right.

As luck would have it, wind and wave had subsided to some degree. Sky cleared to the south and Brad, after warming the engine, gave all his command. The pontoons wallowed deep in dark water, slowly rising, the spray obliterating all beyond. Finally the pontoons crease wave tops and after a run of nearly a mile, parted company with the lake.

Brad worked the plane to altitude and we plodded along at 95 miles an hour. About 15 minutes went by when Jim said, "Are those lights straight ahead?"

"They sure are," Brad chuckled. "We're in luck. The sky's opened up and they're the lights strung around the open pit iron ore mines on the west ridge about Schefferville."

"Are you kiddin'?" Jim said. "Schefferville must be 60 or 70 miles away."

"No," Brad answered, "I've seen them before as far away as we are now. In less than an hour, we'll be in."

True to his word, Brad was soon circling for a landing.

"Brad," I said, "how can you see to land?"

"Those 100-watt bulbs on the crib put a shimmer on the water. I'll get down."

I smiled and said, "That's not what I mean. I know you'll get down, but if you come in too hard, the floats will go under, rip the undercarriage off or flip the plane. I don't want to play submarine."

Brad laughed and said, "Take it easy old man, you want to live forever?"

"No," I said, "just through this landing."

Brad came down the incline and leveled off; the plane, still dropping, skipped lightly on the surface. Then, the pontoons dug in slowly, and eventually the plane came to a near stop.

Jim, who had been quiet, spoke up, "Beautiful landing, Brad, just beautiful."

"All my landings are beautiful," Brad replied.

GOODBYE... NEVER

I was the last to leave home. Father and mother died within a four-month span and after their passing I did not tarry long - too many ghosts.

Several years have slipped by and yet I know now the old house will intrude on my thoughts forever. Fifty-three years of living cannot be swept aside. It has been said, "Life is just a bowl of cherries," but with the sweet are found the sour.

However, the tide of fond memories all but blots out the sad.

In 1925, a few years after completion of the house, we moved in. It was a small two-story box of a house, colonial yellow with white trim and often in need of paint in depression dark years. There were no imposing structures on the block. It fitted the setting. Professional builders had no hand in the construction. A man who lived up the street and a helper, little more than a boy, pieced it together, but theirs was honest workmanship.

When 90 mile-an-hour winds of a coastal hurricane battered our little bastion, although it snapped and shuddered with each angry blast, it did not yield. In the backyard some 60 feet away was a row of Lombardy Poplars that screened a high bank. At the storm's crescendo, the top of one tree sheared off and struck the house, taking a small bite from one corner of the roof before ricocheting butt-end down to punch a hole in the garage. The damage was quickly patched and the normal pattern of life resumed.

We lived on a steep hill. The tar and stone side street was shaded in summer by the crowning glory of American poplars, white elms, and sugar maples. Much of the sidewalk was red brick and the roots of the towering trees heaved the walk and on occasion, in my haste at play or errand-bound, it caused a tumble.

Three square columns supported the front porch roof and between them, a lattice work which my brother and I found convenient for climbing. It almost led to my downfall one summer night. Sent to my room for some infraction of family code, I found the urge to join the boys at play irresistible. Opening my front bedroom window, I dropped to the porch roof and scrambled down the lattice. My extended play period was enjoyed.

However, finding the house strangely quiet for some length of time, my father did some checking. On returning to my room I was greeted with an ultimatum: the next two evenings would be spent at home.

Now and then I pass the old homestead and am once again caught up in a parade of wonderful yesterdays, like the memory of our curly-haired Airedale, "Ginger," rising from the porch deck to wag his stub tail in greeting as I bounded up the front steps on return from school.

Many times I was lulled to sleep by dancing leaves and fingering branches of a large poplar that brushed the clapboards when nudged by a southern breeze, a breeze that bore in May the fragrance of lilac that grew in gay profusion around the house.

The old house had time to know us well. She tolerated two rambunctious boys who, among other things, broke a few windows - primarily with baseballs - as we played catch in the yard. Father would scold, but because he had a liking for baseball (a sport he participated in with some degree of proficiency in his youth) there was no laying on of hands. Out of mother's hearing, he would give us another lecture on lack of control.

The house listened to grace over meager Depression meals on a squeaky dining room table. Although food was in short supply, it seemed to last longer at suppertime as we related affairs of the day. There were arguments, too, but respect and understanding transcended the minor problems of spirit and ego.

I remember father on cold winter mornings shaking down the coal furnace and drafting it to get some semblance of warmth in three small bedrooms. The burning coal also created a removal problem - shoveling ashes from pit to metal containers and then lugging them to the street at collection time.

The house saw my brother's departure in the first draft before Pearl Harbor, and mine later in the conflict. On return, she sheltered us as he recovered from wounds and I went back to school. In due time my brother moved away accepting a position in another city.

Even though the house had shortcomings - small rooms with one overhead light, narrow stairs, and wallpaper that had served beyond its time - the basic comforts were there.

The day came. The old house was sold. It wasn't worth much . . . monetarily.

JOBS NOT TO HAVE

As a kid during the Great Depression, I remember working with a landscaper for 25 cents an hour, later graduating to 50 cents as a county road gang member. It was a time when one was lucky to have a few coins in one's pocket.

When young, little heed is given to the danger involved in work details. Tasks can be confronted without thought of bodily harm. If a touch of the serious side comes to mind, it may be more like whistling past the cemetery. Even in my somewhat carefree attitude, eventually it dawned on me that inherent danger was waiting in the wings. What was expected of workers on construction projects involved danger from start to end of day.

Working on brush gangs, clearing timber for gas lines, presented some problems. There were no chainsaws at the time, so 2-man saws, axes, and bush shears were the order of the day. Years later, with the advent of the chainsaw, the danger was far greater. On one project, the branch of a falling tree nicked me, and a fellow nearby gashed his upper leg down to the bone with an idling chainsaw. With several men cutting timber and the right of way crisscrossed by felled trees whose trunks were propped up several feet by branches, you had to use the trunks as escape routes.

Long ago I remember seeing an article in The Reader's Digest listing gas lines as the most dangerous construction of all. Having worked on several, I do not doubt that conclusion. One line running from Tennessee to New York State was called the "Big Inch." I think the gauge was the largest at the time. On the project was a 60-ton machine that could bend cold pipe. I saw one pipe bent 27 degrees. The process created quite a racket.

The most dangerous job on the line was attaching cable to the pipe and riding it back to the bender. This I found to be a precarious detail. The pipe, up to 45 feet in length, had the center and degree of bend marked. The pipes were set on 4 by 6 skids and, after attaching cable to the center, the winch on a 16-ton bulldozer with counter weights would suck it up. The "swamper," as the rider was called, sat on one end and by so doing, the far end would be elevated. The swamp clamped knees and kept feet up so as not to get them crushed as the dozer moved to the bender. The back of the pipe would thump the ground lightly. After getting the pipe in the machine and angle made, it was returned to the same spot. The bender would be moved sporadically so that pipe could be drawn by 2 dozers and fed from both sides.

One day as I rode pipe, a recently-hired young fellow got between 2 pipes; as one was lifted it swung toward the other, and ⅞-inch beveled pipes came together and cut his right leg off below the knee, and also the ends of 3 fingers on his right hand. The swamper made a mistake but so did the dozer driver. The winch should never have been started with an angled cable and the man between the pipes.

Accidents were too prevalent. One day after a thunderstorm, there were puddles left on the right of way. A flatbed truck with a load of pipe was moving slowly down the line when the wheels directly behind the left side of the cab hit a puddle and dropped, as if there was no road there. The abrupt stop shifted the whole load forward, crushing the cab and killing the driver.

One day after a shower, the bender was being eased down a slope. The thin layer of dirt, being wet and over solid shelf rock, did not hold. I do not recollect whether dozer in front of the bender jack-knifed but the 60-ton monster broke loose and rolled down the mountainside. Sometimes men would save steps by riding the machine. Luckily that was not the case, thank heaven.

Crossing a river, pipe was being fastened a few feet out from a railroad bridge. One morning a welder walking the pipe fell into the river. He was hastily fished out, founded to be in good shape, and so returned to work.

Wagon drills and dynamite were used in rock and even in swamps where expansive shallow V's were made to get pipe down. On one gas line, fuse dynamite was used early on but soon changed possibly due to an accident. A backhoe operator came close to going to the land beyond. He started to clear ditch after the explosion but the fuse on one stick was still smoldering and it blew showering him with debris. He was pock-marked with stone but suffered no serious injury to his face. He was patched up and returned to work in a matter of days.

Swamps were rip-rapped with trees and brush so that dozers could work right through. As I was standing with a 4-by-6 skid on the edge of the riprap waiting for a dozer to pass, it flipped the loose end of the log my 5-foot skid was on. The skid close to my body shot up, as my hand fell off it, narrowly missing my chin but hitting the peak of my baseball cap, flipping it off. The skid rose high in the air and I thought to myself, had it been closer to my body, my chin might have been struck with serious injury resulting.

Another dangerous detail involved unloading pipe from 36 railway cars to paddled beams or flatbed trucks when available. The cars were on a siding with the New York Central main line running along one side. I would attach heavy bent plate steel hooks to ends of pipe that stretched the whole length of the car. The crane operator would swing pipes, while I dropped off the car to release them on trucks or beams, where they would slowly roll away, clearing the immediate area. Twice one morning, as pipes were slowly lifted, the wind caught them and to get clear, jimmying down to the NYC tracks was the only alternative.

The most dangerous problem evolved one day after lunch. There was a 2-man crew with the crane, an operator, and an "oiler," as he was called. The oiler not only lubricated the machine but checked maintenance. When lunchtime came, they went to a nearby town to eat. On returning, the operator got into the cab to move the crane into position while I mounted another load of pipe. The crane ended up farther away from the pipe than usual and when he started the lifting procedure with a low boom, the pipe hesitated in flight and came crashing down. It escaped the hooks and flew off the car.

I scrambled to safety, avoiding the pipe and other pipes shifting from the blow. I look at the crane and noticed one side was off the ground and if the boom hadn't come to rest on the car, the crane would have turned over. With a low boom the leverage was too great. The reason for the disaster became evident when I saw the oiler assisting a not-too-stable operator from the machine. It was easy to see why the accident happened – the operator was drunk. Much of his lunch had been of the liquid variety. Drink was not conducive to his or my welfare. The oiler righted the machine, putting pressure on the boom, then convinced the operator no more work would be done that day, and he was taken home.

The "Big Inch" was exhausting beyond labor; it was a 6 AM start and 6 PM finish if lucky. The foreman, welders, powder men, and operators of heavy equipment would get bonuses if the line was finished ahead of schedule. At least a mile of pipe was to be in the hole every day. It was tough keeping up when going through swamp and rock. Too frequently, suppers were on hold and work not stopped until vehicle lights had been utilized for some time. All you could do on return to lodging was shower, eat, and sleep. Workweeks were always 6 and sometimes 7 days. Overtime came on Thursday and often sooner.

I was glad to leave my detail with the pipe bender for a short period when the dynamite crew was in need of a man. I became associated with wagon drills, electric caps, and 30 or 40 percent gelatin dynamite. I sensed there was a reason for a raise in pay concerning the job.

While building a road, I had the task of keeping the paving material level in the hopper of the machine that spread a strip of road. Walter Snow Fighter trucks would back up and fill the hopper. However, the result was a pile of tar and stone much higher in the center. With a short handled shovel I would work the material back and forth so a full strip would result. It was not an easy task as the machine was moving toward me while I constantly backed up. Down low on the hopper was a 2x4 strip as a guard to keep a foot from getting caught under the machine.

Then one day, this safety measure was tested and came up short. My foot was in a depression so the toe of my shoe did not come in contact with the board. I did not realize the problem until I felt pressure on my arch. I lucked out because of several factors. At the time, the weather had been running into the 90's, so the rough layer of larger tar and stone underneath was a bit soft and my foot was forced back to some degree, although held fast. Also, the driver of the spreader was looking right at me, perhaps realizing the danger inherent in the job, and he shut the machine down so I did not lose a foot. My foot was very sore for a few months but I continued working and had no more harrowing experiences on that project.

When recalling the jobs held in the distant past, it seemed danger was everywhere. There was almost a total disregard for safety. I am thankful that positive changes have been made through the years allowing many workers to live a healthy, long life. Conditions were certainly different when I was young, but danger on construction projects is still with us today.

TIME AND THE CARIBOU

No human stain marked the land. The trails that interlaced it were those of the caribou, and here on the edge of the Barrens they roamed for centuries. It was their domain and yet not entirely, for over it all hung the omnipresent shadow of the wolf.

A river ran cold and clear north to the sea. Near the bank on the sill of shade from sparse tamarack a mother caribou and her calf grazed silently on the mossy floor. The old cow stopped and listened intently. She had not lived these many years without unending vigilance. Her eyes swept an expanse flecked by sun and shadow looking for the terror-striking form of a wolf. Satisfied that danger was not imminent, the grazing resumed, but not for long.

Caribou are the wanderers of the north. Perhaps it is the instinctive fear of the wolf that drives them on. The old cow prodded the tiny calf and together they sifted through a patch of arctic cotton, crossed a well-defined esker, and then swung into a devil's net of tag alders that guarded the river's edge. The calf, all legs and not too stead, stumbled several times but eventually penetrated the maze.

The overhung bank covered with small blueberry bushes screened the matted, dead vegetation that intertwined with tag alder roots. It was one of nature's traps. Now on the brink the cow's right foreleg broke through and dangled in mid-air. She pitched forward, caught herself and struggling, bellied off the bank to the shallows below. The calf followed without incident. Had the cow been moving faster, her hindquarters would have whipped around and hung down over the water. Then she might not have escaped the trap and slow starvation would have followed. But, life in this severe land is always hanging in the balance.

Here the river was less than 300 yards wide. Nature's plow, the great ice break-up, changed the contour of the river bottom from year to year. However, caribou for generations had crossed on the gravel bar that was the pitch of rapids a quarter mile down river.

Below the pitch the river narrowed, ran deep and quickened its pace as it charged won to the boiling cauldron of the great rapids.

The calf, after sliding off the bank, stood transfixed in the moving water and listened to the rapid's ancient song - still strong through a thousand years. As its mother drew away, the calf hurried to catch up. They passed midstream. The flow became stronger. The bend of river above created a heavier thrust to the far side and that thrust had dug a deeper channel. The calf braced hard against the current. Now the gap was 50 yards, but the calf was getting low in the water. It stepped on a small rock not firmly imbedded in the bottom, and like a hair trigger, the rock turned over beneath its weight. The calf dropped lower in the water and floated free. Panic-stricken, the animal struck for bottom, but to no avail. Hooves skated over gravel on the downside of the bar and then lost all contact. Now the calf was in the grip of the unyielding river. One quick glance at her bleating baby drifting fast away, and the mother splashed shoreward. She crashed through a wall of tag elders and headed for a rock ledge barely 200 yards above white water. Reaching the ledge, she poised for a moment as if to judge the speed of the drifting calf.

Then suddenly she jumped and began to slice the heavy current. Swimming slightly behind its path as she neared her offspring, she whirled around just in time. The Swimming slightly behind its path as she neared her offspring, she whirled around just in time. The calf slapped hard against its mother's side and held for a moment. Trying to hold back the calf, she lost ground. The jaws of the great rapid were close at hand—a seething maelstrom that would mercilessly pound them and suck them over the falls to certain death on the rocks below.

The cow, with the calf on her upstream side, swam determinedly for shore as the roar of the cataract grew louder and louder. Finally she found her footing on the river bottom, and tin moments, cow and calf scrambled safely to shore. On the Labrador bank in a saddle carpeted with caribou moss, they huddled together to rest from their ordeal and to renew strength for the trail ahead.

Eventually they wandered on, grazing from time to time in mossy aisles between stunted tamarack and spruce. A Labrador Jay flushed from a blueberry patch and startled them, but what followed froze the mother caribou in her tracks. They herd the distant eerie cry of a wolf and then the answer call of another. No sound is more frightening to a caribou. All problems were now one. The mother butted the calf into instant flight.

The wolf, a persistent hunter and nature's dominant force in this harsh land, allowed its prey few mistakes. Now there were two wolves close at hand. Each could drag down a full-grown bull but might suffer some battle scars in the process. On the other hand, a calf could be dispatched quickly and without risk of injury to the attacker.

Up a gentle slope, over a rocky spine, and down the far side the caribou ran. The old cow wheeled around a windfall and almost went down as a thin layer of moss and soil tore loose from solid perma-frost underneath. To the calf the headlong flight was new, yet it was old as time itself. Ahead, gleaming in the sun, lay the waters of a long narrow lake. Water had always been the caribou's salvation. Now a half-mile away it beckoned. At the bottom of the slope the hard trail turned soft. Cow and calf floundered on a small level waste of muskeg. Mud and Hassocks quivering under the hoof, slowed them down. The caribou emerged on the far side of the muskeg, their bodies punished by their struggle.

They were spurred on by the howl of a wolf close behind. Monuments of rocks, like tombstones, lay ahead: no certitude of direction as they threaded through. Now with sanctuary near at hand, the gate closed. A mass of rocks faced them. They pilled in panic for a moment against the sheer wall then moved along it. A cleft was found: however the irregular break showed no clear passage. They would look no further for out of the shadows, not 40 yards away, two gray forms appeared. Mother pushed calf into the opening and closed behind. They were committed to a deadly trap or escape. The hoped-for avenue of deliverance narrowed. Calf passed easily between rocky walls but mother caught for a moment then slipped by. A wolf tore at her hindquarters. She lashed out with splay-hoof catching the wolf full on the chest slicing it open and flipping the animal backward. He regained his feet and came on. The cow burst through to a narrow sand spit.

Just ahead, the calf had stopped in the shallows and looked back apprehensively. Mother almost swept past, but managed to slow to protect the calf. The injured lead wolf had swung off and was charging down on easy prey, the seemingly defenseless calf, only to be met by the cow's shoulder. The wolf bounced off into the water, and before it recovered, mother and calf had quickly gained deep water scant feet ahead of the hungry wolves. Thwarted in their attempt to get calf or mother, the wolves watched, belly-deep in water, tongues lolling, eyes fastened on what was to be their dinner. However, this day they would not dine on caribou.

In the chain of events the weak link had been the calf. Now it was the old cow. At the point of entry, the lake was little more than a mile wide, a caribou in its prime could swim five times that distance without trouble. But the cow was old, near exhaustion from the river fight and frenzied run from wolves. Fate, the eternal hunter, could still play a dark hand.

Alone and tired, the young calf could never make the far shore. Strangely enough, although the calf was completely dependent, nevertheless it would hardly show or hinter the crossing. Nature would remedy this problem.

As the mother swam slowly out into the lake, the calf instinctively nestled in behind placing head on mother's rump. There it was safe, little chance to tire and have head drop in water and drown. Also the curl of water behind the mother created a back eddy that was helping to pull the calf along.

They progressed slowly forward what, for the mother, was a distant shore. The middle of the lake was reached. Strength drained, taxed severely, the old cow fought on. Self-preservation is strong in all animals, but stronger still was this mother's protective instinct for her offspring. She could feel the head still resting on her rump and occasionally a leg thumping against hers and it gave strength. Glass eyes focused on the shore - slower, ever closer - the bottom was underfoot. The tortuous swim was over.

Flame of life flickering low, movement fraught with pain, she labored ashore and dropped into a bed of fireweed. She lay flat and wheezing for breath. Death had borrowed greatly from life.

The frightened calf nestled close and waited. Some time passed before the old cow's head came up. She nuzzled the baby at her flanks. A loon's sad lament at departing day mutes a white crowned sparrow's song. The distant mournful cry of a hungry wolf drifts across the lake. Shadows flood in and night once again possess the land. From the horizon, northern lights mound and roll in undulating waves across the sky. The little calf stares in wonder. The age-old struggle would go on, but for now cow and calf were safe.

POT OF GOLD TURNED OUT TO BE FRIENDS

It is with great satisfaction that I recall the warmth of friendships past. In my early days, the Great Depression was on the land. Meals were basic, portions small, and clothing went through a hand-me-down routine. However, the fine decent people of the neighborhood denied the gloom of depression years.

It seemed there was little thought of the battle ahead, but positive uplifting measures from day to day. Certainly hardship brought forth unsuspected coverage to stay the course. Some people are best when challenged. Energy is liberated in constructive ways. Material things were nearly non-existent. However helping hands were always present. No doubt appreciation for small favors coming time after time built fence around adversity. Faith held fast and deep consideration for friends developed.

The odds faced were great, but several families had a far greater burden to carry due to loss of fathers struck down by heart attacks and other illnesses when the children were young. One boy much younger than his two brothers was placed in the House of Providence, that being an orphan's home. The mother had to work and the lad was too young to fare for himself. A few years later he returned to the family. It was truly remarkable that the women who headed these fatherless households persevered under such adverse conditions. I do not remember complaints but smiles when I pounded on doors gathering friends to play.

We did not want for activity. Although there were no outdoor basketball courts or indoor ones around and Pop Warner football as well as Little League baseball were non-existent, we were involved. Household chores were attended to but ample time was found for playing fields and to roam wide-open spaces. We played football, baseball, and hockey and gravitated to streams and woodlands. When hockey was on the agenda, we traveled a long mile to a pond where many fine invigorating games gook place. Sometimes the puck would escape and end up near the stream end. Once I tried to rescue one on thin ice there and found out swimming in winter was not enjoyable. No matter the weather, the games continued. When necessary not only sticks and skates were carried but shovels as well.

From the neighborhood evolved so many constructive people. Whether prominent or not, all became assets to community and country. Pat Bright, owner of Dunk & Bright furniture and Letterman of Distinction at Syracuse University, now lives on East Lake Road.

Herb Leary became a well-known surgeon and lectured at AMA conventions. Keith Shinaman was pastor of the Presbyterian Church in Marcellus for 36 years and a member of the National Presbyterian Church governing board for 12 years. His younger brother, David, managed the accounting staff at Welch Allyn as controller for 20 years and lived in Skaneateles. He now lives in Williamsburg, VA, with wife, Marilyn, who retired as pastor there but continued her ministry as chaplain of a retirement complex.

It is pleasing to see following generations that emulate parental character and are successful in chosen field of endeavor. David and Marilyn have two sons, Jeff and Todd, and a daughter, Amy. The boys graduated from Cornell and Ohio State. Jeff is presently the vice president of Saratoga Springs Chamber of Commerce. Todd and his wife are both attorneys in Rochester. Amy, who lives in Skaneateles, married Andy Nye from Marcellus. She graduated from St. Lawrence as did her dad, and is presently a busy housewife and mother attending two young daughters. Andy is an electrical engineer at Welch Allyn.

More and more in my advancing years I find myself lost in the passing parade of youthful memories. Lessons were learned on playing fields and though household chores. More important was the steadfastness, the will to succeed, handed down by parents. They imbued their children with standards of conduct and character that stayed the years. I guess you could say parents were realists, yet always there was a touch of optimism. They were not common, but uncommon people. Moral integrity was there and they passed it on. They were on the same page, true to the light within and they knew of meaning beyond self that gave their limited days definition and direction.

BEHIND THE MONUMENT

Saturday morning on Memorial Day weekend in Borodino, a fine tribute was paid to all servicemen and women, living and dead, who fought on land, sea and air, in defense of freedom.

Underlying this event is another story. Without a wonderful outpouring of warm hearts and helping hands, the monument and enhancement of the surrounding area, could not have been accomplished. These constructive, dedicated individuals alleviated considerable expense. Costs incurred would have been prohibitive when considering certain problems like architecture, survey and design. The utilization of an old well and water lines for garden and other uses would have been expensive as well. Sal Strod, an architect from Skaneateles, donated his time, as did Paul Hood who made the survey. The designing of the monument, a major task was undertaken by Dr. Fritelli. Joyce Green's father connected well with water lines. Ryan Phillips, a 17-year-old lad from Marcellus, lined up money to be acquired from a water ski trip the length of Skaneateles Lake. This was accomplished and the result was splendid sum of about $2,000.

Other problems although not major in scope, were still of great importance. Without grading and topsoil, difficulties would arise concerning grass, flowers, shrubs and trees. A beautiful perennial garden with rare flowers was planted along with shrubs, evergreen and birch trees. World famous Mt. Airy granite for benches and the splendid monument - an obelisk - was shipped in from North Carolina. Overall, a very capable committee undertook a time-consuming task and kept things in good order. They deserve a great deal of credit.

By no means should so many others who gave time and effort be over looked. In an incredible display of generosity, veterans, their families and a large number of people not directly linked to the military, were heavily involved, monetarily as well. The people of Spafford and others surely answered the call. As one old veteran, I thank you. God bless one and all.

ALMOST HOME

Swept by an early morning breeze, a white veil of mist was rising from New York Harbor. It was the first calm day in over a week and a welcome relief from the late November storm.

The 12,500-ton Sea Tiger, a ballast free cargo ship, presently a troop transport, had been pounded mercilessly all the way across the Atlantic. Almost to a man, we had been seasick and now, with the ship on an even keel, weak and haggard men flooded the deck, pressing against the crowded rail, yearning for their land again.

Suddenly, off the port side towering above the mist, the Statue of Liberty appeared. Men's eyes strained to see the symbol and stood in awe, stunned and silent. Someone found his sound and shouted, "There she is! There she is!"

With reverent silence broken slowly across the crowded rail, the murmur of voices, like an onrushing wave, rose to a crescendo and then trailed off.

On my right, a few shoulders away, I could hear a man say, "I never thought I'd see her again."

And nearby the question, "Why do ya say that?"

In a choked and halting voice he replied, "Most of you guys were in Africa and Italy up to two and a half years. I don't deny that is a long time to be away from home, but before we entered the war I went to Canada and got into a volunteer unit. We trained for a while, then shipped to England and after a little more preparation pushed on to Africa. There were times in the desert - fighting with the British against Rommel's Afrika Korps - that I didn't think I'd see another day. Back and forth trading victories . . . Bardia, Tobruk, Benghazi. I remember one town traded hands six times. Through sandstorms, heat, and of course the ever-present deviltries of man, land mines, bombs, the guns of tanks and massed artillery - almost two years passed before you fellows arrived."

He hesitated for a moment, and then, casting a fleeting glance at the great lady fading from view astern he murmured low, "No, I never thought I'd see her again."

He turned from the rail, saying then that he felt tired. Suddenly his knees buckled, hands clutching the rail fell free. Now he lay on deck gasping for breath, and pained and questioning expression on his face. Then he lost consciousness. Some of the men quickly lifted and carried him to sickbay.

To the muffled throb of propeller and engines we slowly proceeded up the Hudson River to Camp Shanks and anchored offshore. Waiting was near torture for sick, tired men longing to end their confinement and stand once again on firm ground.

Uneasiness was soon alleviated, however, when ferries came alongside and the transfer of human cargo was made. As troops moved toward ferry slips, Red Cross volunteers distributed cartons of fresh milk, something the men had not tasted since leaving the States. Even though for most, the lasting effects of seasickness might deny the holding of it, the men fell upon it ravenously.

That night we heard news that the soldier stricken on shipboard had died of a heart attack. What kind of justice was this? For four and a half long years he had gone through every conceivable kind of hell. Now with family and friends beckoning, fate - the eternal hunter - had taken him by the hand.

OUT OF THE SHADOWS

Craig moved quickly through the side entrance and pressed close to the right wall of the corridor as he proceeded toward the fifth grade classroom. Opposite the doorway, he bolted across and stepped inside. Glancing at the empty seats, he breathed a sigh of relief, walked along the wall of blackboards to his left and slipped into the last seat. For the moment he would not worry about prying eyes.

Students began to trickle in, then a tall, slender woman in her mid-thirties with honey blonde hair came through the door and strode firmly to her desk. Craig had been told his teacher would be Miss Lane. There were few vacant seats when the late bell rang.

Miss Lane introduced herself, then, with seating chart in hand, set about arranging the students alphabetically. Down the first row she went, where Craig sat cowering in the corner with head turned toward the wall. He stared in fright with his left eye. She took another step to his side, looked up and said, "You are new - " but the sentence was never finished. Mouth open, wide-eyed, she stared at the right side of his face. Covering it from temple to jaw was a reddish purple blotch, a birthmark. Recovering somewhat from the shock, she stammered, "You . . . you are new here?"

He looked up at her sorrowfully through his eyebrows, his inner self dominating his face and eyes. "Yes, if I was here last year you would remember."

Miss Lane, now in control of her faculties, said, "There are enough desks so I am going to leave the last seat in every row vacant. I will place you in another seat."

Craig brushed a lock of brown hair back; gray eyes pleaded with her as he asked, "Can I please stay here?"

"Yes, I guess that can be arranged."

His mouth opened but he swallowed the words and nodded his gratitude. Miss Lane acknowledged it with a smile.

The girl seated in front of Craig looked on as she circled the back of the room and moved to her assigned seat. For a moment she covered her face with her hands and then whispered to the girl ahead. The buzzing swept across the room as Craig and the teacher spoke.

Seating finished, Miss Lane oriented the class as to subject matter, time periods, other teachers that would instruct them. The only outside instruction would be in art, physical education, and music.

In midmorning the music teacher appeared. Miss Lane hastened to the office and confronted Mrs. Dutton, the secretary. "Why wasn't I notified about the new boy, Craig Gentry?"

"Oh, I must apologize. You were in the teachers' meeting yesterday when Mrs. Gentry came to register the boy. Later in the confusion it slipped my mind."

"He does have quite a problem. I may have hurt him more. It startled me and he certainly noticed my reaction. I feel so sorry for him. Do you have the home phone number?"

"Yes, but no one will be there now. His mother works in Warner's Bakery and his father's dead."

"Dead! What happened?"

"He was killed while working in the freight yards - fell under a railroad car. She nearly broke down when I asked for information concerning the emergency card."

"How terrible. When did this happen?"

"Less than a year ago."

"What a blow that must have been. Is Craig the only child?"

"Yes."

"I will call his mother at lunchtime and see if I can find out more about Craig. Thank you, Mrs. Dutton."

Lunchtime came and the call was made.

"I am Craig's teacher, Evelyn Lane."

"I wanted to talk to you, Miss Lane. I only have Craig now and I fear his classmates' reaction to his birthmark. We moved here hoping he might be treated better. School was such a dreadful experience that he didn't want to leave the house. One day he came home crying because the kids didn't want him walking on the same side of my street. They threw snowballs trying to drive him to the other side."

"Children can be cruel sometimes. I will do what I can from this end."

"Thank you. I appreciate your call and concern."

Several days passed, each with its special problems. Wendy Alcott, the girl seated in front of Craig, wanted to be moved. Miss Lane talked with Carl Aronson and he agreed to switch seats. It seemed a good move for one morning before school was in session, she noticed Carl talking to Craig.

Nearly a week had gone by and Craig, still in his own little world, had not contributed anything. Then the fateful day came. Miss Lane questioned him about geography homework.

"Craig, would you name the Great Lakes for us?"

Craig did not rise; his breathing stopped, his chest tightened, but he managed to mutter, "I don't know, Miss Lane."

"Did you do your homework?"

"I . . . no, Miss Lane."

"Then you will stay after school today, Craig."

He did not answer but bowed his head.

When the last bell rang and all the students had left the room except Craig, Miss Lane said, "Come here and sit in front of my desk."

Craig shuffled to the front and seated himself.

"Why did you neglect your homework, Craig?"

He looked up and stammered, "I . . . I did my homework."

"Why tell me otherwise then?"

"I'm sorry to cause trouble. But if I stand up everybody stares at me."

For a moment she said nothing, contemplating his anguish.

"You must face - " she almost choked on the word, "--the problem and give yourself a chance to develop fully, to enjoy life."

He lifted his head, turned the right side of his face toward her for a second as if to jog her memory.

"Craig, you have a healthy body and mind. I will help any way I can, before or after school."

"I would like to stay after school every day, please."

"Why every day?"

"Well . . . I'd rather go home after the others. The kids make fun of me."

"We will try to put a stop to that," she said.

Craig did not say a word but he thought of all the taunts and even fights he had in the last school he attended.

The following day, when the school came to a close, Craig silently seated himself once again before Miss Lane and started to do his homework. A curly-haired Airedale appeared at the door, looked in, then pranced to Craig's side, placed forepaws on his leg and wagged a stubby tail.

"Is that your dog?" Miss Lane asked.

"Yes, my face doesn't bother him. He's the only friend I have."

"Your mother cares for you, Craig. She's a friend and so am I."

"Oh, I meant someone to play with. I didn't mean . . . you have been nice to me. I'll take Ginger out. He usually waits outside. Somebody must have left the door open and he came to find me."

"Ginger can stay if he keeps quiet."

"Thank you. He'll lie down beside me and won't make any noise."

"How old is Ginger?"

"Six." The dog had stirred bright memories of his father. "We lived about a mile from a trout stream before we moved here. My father and I walked there a lot to fish and Ginger would go along too."

Miss Lane saw the sadness in his eyes and understood the longing, the loneliness that lay behind.

Craig continued, "We live on Moreland Avenue now, close to the city limits. Ginger and I go for hikes in the woods and fields, but I wish I had a boy friend," and as if to release some pent-up emotion, blurted out, "I'm not monster, I'm human too."

Miss Lane swallowed hard and said, "Maybe you can strike up a friendship with Carl Aronson who sits in front of you. He is a fine boy."

"He's the only one that has spoken to me."

"Well he may be your friend already. Put your best foot forward and start a conversation now and then."

"I will, Miss Lane."

The following day after lunch, Miss Lane noticed Craig was in a state of blackest despondency. When the dismissal bell rang, Craig did not stay as usual but moved toward the door. Miss Lane called to him. As he came close he said, "I'd rather not stay today."

"What is the trouble, Craig?"

"I don't try to make enemies but I have them."

A tear coursed down his cheek. He pulled a sleeve across his face and blurted out, "I'm sorry."

"No need to apologize for being human. What happened?"

"I went to the cafeteria to eat my sandwich. Two boys were at one table. I sat as far away from them as possible. Both got up and one said, 'Why don't you wear a mask?' Miss Lane, I'm worried about the future. What will I do in the years ahead? You go to school to learn so you can get a job. Why try anymore? No one will want me."

Miss Lane was finding it hard to control herself, as she was maddened by Craig's experience. The mind had been given so many dark images. But, she thought to herself, she must not let the spark go out.

She rose, walked around the desk, and placed a hand on his shoulder. He recoiled slightly and looked up at her.

"Why did you jump when I touched you?"

"It startled me. No one touches me. I'm poison."

"You are not poison. The young are affected more by such things. They haven't seen much of the world and they do not understand your problem." The depth of his hurt stunned her.

Suddenly, he seemed compelled to speak of things that had been cooped up in his troubled mind. "But the first day when you were seating the class, you looked at me as if you'd seen a ghost."

"Yes, but mainly because of my concern for you."

She changed the subject. "What do you do in your spare time, Craig?"

"I take walks in the country. There are all kinds of birds and animals to see and I like to read books my father had when he was young. Most are stories of the wilderness."

"I have a wilderness book you might enjoy." She stepped to the bookcase and handed the book to Craig. "It is a story based in Alaska."

He clapped the book with both hands. "Thank you," he said, but the real thanks was deep in his eyes.

"You can keep it as long as you like."

"I will return it in a few days."

"You know, Craig, you have a good command of the language. Probably because of your reading. Your English mark should be higher and arithmetic needs improvement too."

"I know, I haven't tried very hard."

"Mr. Farrell said you do well in art class. Why not work on some sketching in your spare time? You owe it to yourself."

Miss Lane thought she saw a slight smile trace his face.

Craig said, "I have a drawing in my notebook of a pheasant in the corn. Would you like to see it?"

"Yes, very much so." She viewed the picture. "This is wonderful. You do have talent."

He took strength with each word and when they walked from the school together he was happy Miss Lane had praised his work.

As days and weeks went by, the aggression shown toward Craig calmed, due primarily to a dedicated Miss Lane, and most of the dark thoughts that stirred in his troubled mind slowly drifted away.

The time came for Craig to leave Miss Lane's class. On the last day, report cards were handed out and class was dismissed. Craig lingered to talk to Miss Lane.

"You should be proud of that report card, Craig," she said.

"I wish my father could see it."

"Your mother will certainly be happy."

"I want to give you this sketch I made of a country scene, Miss Lane. Just a little gift."

"Thank you, Craig, but there was no need." She thought he would not tender the gift before. It might seem like he was looking for a favor. Now it was a simple gift, pure, honest, no stain of subterfuge.

Craig said, "You were my only friend for some time and I know you had a lot to do with me having other friends like Carl Aronson. Sometimes I wonder where I'd be . . ." Eyes clouded as he said, "I will miss you."

"I will miss you too, Craig, more than you know. You are going to make your own tracks now. However, if it can help, I will always be available. Come back and see me anyway."

"I will, Miss Lane." He turned and walked slowly toward the door.

Miss Lane, misty eyed, watched until he disappeared from view. She said to herself, "And I worried all my life about a birthmark on my shoulder."

DESTINATION: LIFE

Only two more hours of daylight and the fishing party still waiting for the flight to Spruce River Lodge a hundred and forty miles away. Mr. Barker was presently entertaining his wife Liz, and Mr. and Mrs. Wells with one of his past exploits in the wilderness. The conversation went unheeded by Jim Hanson, guide, as he scanned the darkening sky to the northwest, then kicked a piece of shale with a heavy leather boot. Ten minutes ago, Jim and Brad Owens, pilot for Horizon Air Services, had loaded the Otter Float Plane that nestled against the crib.

The door of the Operations Shack slammed. Jim turned to see Brad move briskly down the slope toward the waiting plane. Noticing Jim's anxious look he said, "Manager and I had a little problem about tomorrow's schedule." Without hesitation he jumped on the float, hoisted himself to the controls, and shouted, "Let's get this airborne!"

Jim studied the young couples as they moved to board. He smiled inwardly as he said to himself, "Chet and Ellen Wells sure won't keep the plane from flying. Doubt she weighs 110 pounds and he not 30 more."

Liz Barker, a tall, slender woman, pressing a red ski cap tot a crown of blonde hair, was assisted up the aluminum ladder. She seated herself on one of the canvas-covered chairs fastened to the plane. Ellen Wells, her dark eyes flashing with anticipation, clambered up, followed by the two men. Jim held the wing strut while a dockhand unfastened the float, coiled the rope, and tossed it into the tail compartment. Jim hopped aboard as the plane was nosed away from crib. The motor coughed to life and they taxied slowly out into the lake.

Seated on a pile of duffel on the right side of the fuselage, Jim relaxed for a moment. He plucked a faded blue baseball cap from his head, ran fingers through his sparse, gray hair, and then checked the safety belts. Ellen Wells, adjusting hers, looked at Jim. "You're not safe sitting on that luggage."

Jim smiled, "I'm expendable."

Brad twisted around, looked through the opening where you would expect a door to be, and questioned the passengers. "Anyone want to ride up front?"

John Barker was quick to respond. "I'd like to get a few pictures even if it is a little overcast." He unfastened his seat belt and moved forward, camera dangling from a strap around his neck.

Jim knew Barker was a freelance writer for fishing magazines and intent on getting an article. He heard him mention it to all within earshot while picking up the party at Dorais Air Terminal, a few miles from the float base at Wolf Lake.

Looking at the passengers, he was glad they had taken his advice and made the change to fishing togs at the base. Getting in and out of the floatplanes, especially in the bush, could be a problem. The jackets had already been useful while waiting for the flight to temper a light northwest wind and late August subarctic temperatures. The over-the-ankle leather boots, wool socks, and caps would prove their worth many times before the trip was over.

Jim was aroused from his thoughts by the engine's roar. Satisfied the motor was warm, Brad was starting his takeoff run. The pontoons, running deep, ploughed water and gradually rose, a veil of white spray shutting out all beyond. The metallic beat quickened, as the plane skipped on the crests of waves, then was airborne. After gaining necessary altitude to clear western hills, Brad made a heading for camp. Ellen Wells looked at Jim and shouted over the clamor. "How high are we?"

"Two thousand feet."

"Will we go any higher?"

"Doubt it," Jim replied.

Mr. Wells asked, "How long will it take to get there?"

"We're going' about a hundred miles an hour. There's some headwind; hour and a half should do it.

Ellen Wells resumed watching the landscape below. It was a multicolored landscape of Caribou Moss, thinly dotted with Spruce and Tamarack. Tag alders bordered the myriad shorelines of rivers and lakes. As far as the eye could see it was the same.

A half hour went by. The few shafts of sunlight that had pierced the cloud cover were gone and ominous dark clouds, lower than the others, were dead ahead. Brad leaned forward over the controls to get a better view. Although many miles away, he could see they were advancing on a wide front. Disgusted, he wrenched the earphones off, brushed a wisp of straight brown hair from over his right eye and leaned back in his seat. He checked the gauges, then the horizon, hoping the dark cloud mass was an apparition. It was still there. Jaw set, half under his breath he said, "Dammit," and turned to John Barker. "Would you trade places with Jim?" And without waiting for a reply, "Get him up here as soon as possible."

Rising reluctantly from the co-pilot's seat, he shuffled toward the tail of the plane. Jim saw him coming.

"Brad wants to see you."

Jim uncoiled his spare six-foot-three-inch frame, eased past the stout Mr. Barker, entered the compartment, and carefully seated himself. "I see your problem," he said before Brad could speak.

"Yeah, it's really mounting up. Threads of lightning all across the damn thing. Ceiling's right down on the hills. Going to head north. Looks better that way."

He banked the Otter sharply. Jim told the passengers of Brad's intention and quickly returned.

For several minutes they rode the flowing mantle of the storm. Brad dropped the Otter to five hundred feet and was following a large river that coursed its way north to the sea. Peering straight ahead through the windshield, he shouted, "Can't get around this mess. I'm taking it down."

"You know best," Jim replied.

The curtain of rain advancing over the hills to the left would soon encompass them. Brad started to circle the plane.

"The river's wide here. I think I can drop it in."

Reflecting the brooding clouds, the river was now a dark, fluent wound in the wilderness. Circling lower, he took one more quick swing, looking for rocks that might impede the landing. Jim hurriedly shifted to his former perch atop the duffel. Here with the passengers, he could help calm their fears and, from his vantage point on the right side of the fuselage, appraise the situation. It was difficult to see much, with the water dark and ripped by wind just ahead of the storm. Lightning flashed to the west. A few drops of rain streaked the window. There were getting in none too soon.

Brad leveled off at fifty feet and started his approach. The crosswind lifted the right wing, but the landing had to be made with run of river. They dropped lower, pontoons thumped the top of a wave, skipped several more, and hit again. Drumming slowed, pontoons cut deeper, then struck. Liz Barker screamed. The plane tipped violently forward, twisted to the right, but did not flip over. The propeller slapped the water. Ellen Wells, slumped over in front of her husband, started to straighten up. She felt her husband's hand on her shoulder.

"Are you alright?" he gasped.

"I think so, my face struck something."

Liz Barker, behind the pilot's partition, was holding her head and groaning. John Barker, finding himself without injury, released his seat belt and went to her aid.

His wife, now crying, blurted out, "My forehead hit the partition."

"Thank heaven it was padded," John Barker replied.

Unharmed, Brad managed to cut the engine and all switches.

Without safety belt, Jim had been propelled forward, smashing into the co-pilot's compartment, and was lying unconscious in a pile of baggage. Satisfied he had taken all precautions, Brad stepped over a fishing tackle box and started to strip luggage from Jim.

"God, I hope he isn't seriously hurt," he muttered.

Chet Wells regaining his composure spoke up. "He slammed head-on; neck could be broken."

Jim's eyelids fluttered. Eyes opened but did not track. Eventually, in their wandering, they fell on Brad. A smile traced Jim's face. In little more than a whisper he said, "Trying to get rid of me, old friend?"

Brad smiled too. "How do you feel?"

Jim rolled his head around as he massaged his neck. "I'm in one piece. How are the passengers?"

"Banged up a bit but intact."

"What did we hit?"

"A bar of solid rock just under the surface - tore the left pontoon off."

A grating sound accompanied by a slight shifting of the plane brought the conversation to a halt. The left wing, dragging in the current, ploughed deeper. Water seeped into the fuselage. Liz Barker noticed it first and gave the alarm. "The plane's sinking?"

"It isn't going down yet," Brad replied. "When we lighten the load, it may work free and without the left pontoon turn turtle."

Jim pushed the shore-side door, hoping it wasn't jammed. It opened easily. He dropped to the remaining float, resting on the massive ridge, and spun around to help Liz Barker already in the doorway. Once down, he jumped into the water and bade her follow.

She hesitated for a moment, then plunged in and was led up the incline of rock to where the storm-tossed waves were barely breaking.

"Get to shore," Jim said, then retraced his steps to Ellen Wells waiting for his assistance. Her safety attained, he turned to find Chet Wells thrashing in under his own power. John Barker was given a hand and once again Jim made the journey back. Brad was standing on the float with several pieces of duffel in the doorway. "Better get this stuff ashore - plane's lighter now - afraid it might go downriver."

Hurriedly, they moved the bags. Chet Wells joining in. Two more trips and the plane was clean.

Jim herded the party to a recess in the face of a rock a short distance from the river.

The storm, at its zenith, raged with pent-up fury, but the battered, tired band was still intact and protected for the time being. Jim built a fire and a drying-out period ensued. Although heavily laden with rain, the storm did not last long and the respite was welcome. It was a time to assess physical damage as well as immediate problems confronting them. Chet Wells was attending to his wife's needs with a medical kit supplied by John Barker.

"How is she?" Jim asked.

"She's got a split lip and a small cut on her head."

John Barker and wife were seated on Spruce boughs, backs against the rock face. John, usually talkative, now somewhat subdued, managed to voice the leading question. "What do we do now?"

"That," said Jim, "is something we should decide tomorrow. The shock of the crash is still with us. It would be better to collect our thoughts."

Liz Barker, who had been crying for some time, was staring into the fire, too exhausted to say a word.

Brad spoke. "How is the head, Jim?"

"It aches a little." He changed the subject. "You know that plane bothers me. I'd like to tie it down."

Brad replied, "We're thinking the same thing. The plane can be easily spotted from the air - dammit!"

Jim was deep in thought but Chet Wells, hanging on every word, was quick to question. "What's the matter, Brad?"

"Trying to skirt the storm, I had my hands full - flying on the deck …"

"What are you trying to say?" John questioned.

"I flew about thirty miles off-course and didn't contact the base."

"In other words, they don't know where we are?"

"That's right," Brad acknowledged.

"You make a lot of mistakes," John snapped.

Brad started to open his mouth, but Jim cut in. "Let's not make more problems than we've got."

Chet reiterated, "Hold on, John, things may look better come morning."

John mumbled but made no coherent comment. Jim started chopping a dead windfall and soon spaced a few large sections on the fire. Backed by green pieces, it reflected some heat toward the two couples huddled against the cliff.

Jim spoke, "Try to get some sleep. I'll tend fire." He turned to Brad. "You'd better get some shut-eye too."

Brad nodded, took his sleeping bag, and opened it so that it made a blanket for some of the party to lie upon.

Eventually all settled down. Ellen Wells, head on her husband's shoulder, was already at peace with the wilderness.

The long night was over. Guide and pilot up at first light were hovering around a blackened pot that hung over a blazing fire. Chet stirred, and in doing so, woke up his wife.

"I thought it was a bad dream," she said, "but we are still here."

"Yes, but alive," he said.

The Barkers were last to rise. Liz, more in control of her faculties, looked at the pot.

"Is that tea I smell?"

"Yeah," Brad answered, "tea is one thing we have a wealth of."

"Where did you get it?" she asked.

"Occasionally we have to sit it out because of bad weather, and we like to have a few things on the planes to keep body and soul together. Take a hot cup. Dip it out of the pot."

Spirits brightened as pot was joined by fry pan and bacon was added.

"How did we get the bread?" Ellen asked.

"A little luck," replied Jim, "but let me answer later after we get somethin' in our stomachs."

The breakfast of bacon, bread, and tea was skimpy enough but it had great recuperative powers. Meal finished, Brad began to speak.

"I - I believe this discussion should be opened by me, being responsible for our problems. After the crash I was busy getting switches off, checking injuries, and trying to clear the plane. I doubt the radio would work anyway because of the storm, deep river valley, and trouble lately with the Northern Lights; now we will never know."

"What do you mean we will never know?" John questioned.

"The plane is gone. Probably floated downriver until it filled with water and went to the bottom."

John spoke. "What are we going to do?"

"That will be decided right now. As I mentioned before, we are thirty miles off course. Autumn starts in this country in mid-August and sometimes it snows. Three years ago a foot and a half fell the last few days of the month - not that it lasted, but it grounded all planes. Also food has to be considered. There are some pluses. The planes have survival kits although they are often raided by other pilots, as is the case. Still we have items of great importance."

Jim added, "Beside the two pans there's an axe, sleepin' bag, hot cups, fish knives, knapsack, two ropes, med kit, two waterproof containers of matches, and possibly most important of all, two bottles and one spray can of dope."

"What do you mean by dope?" Liz questioned.

"Insect repellent," Jim replied. "Let me run down the food items. We have tea, two packets of orange drink powder, three pounds of bacon, loaf and a half of bread, three envelopes of dehydrated soup, and a half-pound bar of chocolate. The bacon and bread were supplies for the Lodge."

John reiterated, "What are we going to do?"

Jim replied, "Brad and I believe we should head downriver and cross about seven miles below."

Liz Barker screamed, "How are we going to get across?"

Jim continued, "I've seen that part of the river before. There's a long stretch between rapids and relatively shallow. We figure it can be rafted."

"Wait a minute," said Chet. "How about camps in the vicinity?"

Brad broke in. "The closest camp is sixty miles away. To get there would be an almost impossible task. We would have to cross three major rivers, work around several lakes, and fight muskeg too."

Liz said, "Walking will be difficult for me. A cosmetologist gets little exercise. How about waiting here? Don't they say to stay put when you are lost?"

Brad answered, "Under normal conditions, yes, but remember what I said a moment ago - thirty miles off course, weather, food - we can't wait."

Jim spoke, "As far as food is concerned, we're not in immediate danger. The wilderness will provide some essentials."

"Like what?" Liz asked.

"Fish, for one thing; if we keep close to rivers we'll get all we need."

John was quick to question. "You said rivers - I thought we were going down this one and raft to the other shore, although I don't know why."

"The reason is simply this," Jim replied, "after crossing we travel inland for eight miles. That will take us to the Silver River which flows to the coast about forty miles away."

"What is on the coast?" John asked.

"Artuk, an Eskimo village - actually a few white men there too. They've got a radio station and a landing strip that was used during World War II, and still in service. There's only one slight catch. The village is located on the other side of the river - but when we get to the mouth they'll see us."

He said it as if it was a positive thing. All agree with the plan.

The wind had died along the river. Warmth from the sun had brought a mixed blessing. Black flies were beginning at their work. Pants tucked into wool socks, hats, and dope on exposed parts kept them at bay.

Articles of wearing apparel, some fishing tackle, and hip boots were to be left behind. John questioned the leaving of the boots.

Jim said, "They weren't for walkin'."

John dropped it there.

The sorting continued. More articles were argued over, but eventually the task was done. Brad carried his sleeping bag in a small canvas cover, also a coil of rope over his shoulder and under his arm. John had a medium-sized gym bag in hand. Chet was burdened with two fishing poles and a coil of rope. A knapsack on Jim's back contained pans, foodstuffs, three-piece fishing pole, and in one hand, the axe. Pockets of his field jacket were loaded with smaller articles, as were pockets of the others. Even light rain gear was stuffed inside. Men carried equipment in one hand; the women, none. Better able to fend off insects or tag alders. Ready to go, they gazed with sadness at their little bastion against the storm, turned away, and started the trek downriver with Jim in the lead.

They kept close to the river. The river being low this time of year, it afforded them an opportunity to move at a fair pace and escape blackflies. A mile gained, Jim halted the column.

John Barker spoke. "Why stop now? We just got started."

"We're not takin' a walk in the park. Scramblin' over rocks is hard work."

John still protested. "We will never get to our destination."

Jim, irritated, replied, "I've got the whole party to think about. You don't hurry in this country."

Jim turned his attention to Ellen Wells who had a little coagulated blood on a swollen, split lip, and a splotch of red in her dark hair.

"How ya doin'?"

"Better than I expected, I suppose."

Jim, surprised at the answer, was thankful she was in good spirits.

They moved on until a narrow blind bay penetrating deep into the bush brought them to a halt. Jim, with Brad close behind, waited for the rest of the party.

Jim spoke. "These tag alders grow to water's edge and like to toss ya in the drink. We'll go inland."

Away from the thrust of the river and nature's plow, the great ice breakup, the landscape had not been scoured and tag alders had grown profusely. High overhead they offered little opportunity to see more than a few yards, and their tenacity to impede the passage of persons and equipment was not appreciated. The barrier was not wide and they were soon free of their adversary.

Chet brushed a twig from his jacket and said, "Ellen and I had a few battles with tag alders before, on camping trips. Never could see why the Lord planted them."

An esker was crossed, then for a time they travelled a meadow flecked with Arctic cotton. In the distance a grazing caribou lifted his head and, with trotting horse gait, drifted into the shadows of a thin stand of Tamarack. On an outcropping of rock they rested once more.

"Why are the trees so few and so small?" Ellen asked.

Jim replied, "We're on the edge of the barren ground. You see, the growin' season's little more than two months."

Jim wondered if Ellen's question was more than superficial. Perhaps she was trying to help the others by keeping thoughts away from the more pressing problems.

Brad said, "You seem to be taking the hike well, Ellen."

"Playing tennis two or three times a week may help."

Jim thought to himself, "That's an asset," and then spoke to the party. "I'm gonna ration food. We could go through our supply in three days. Need more time than that."

John questioned, "How long will it take to get to the coast?"

"Depending on problems, five to seven days."

"How long will the rations last?" Chet asked.

"They'll last. May run out of bread but I'll hold the bacon down. Days will be cool and when we hole up at night I can put it on the permafrost. The river will provide. Let's get movin'."

Although the day was cool, sun, exertion, and heavy clothing raised a thirst. Arriving at the riverbank, they drank the cold, crystal clear water with relish and then prepared to eat. Some brook trout and a landlocked salmon were caught. Brad had a fire going between two rocks. A fry pan spanned them and in it, six slices of bacon. All had a slice of bacon and bread. Fish were fried in the fat and tea washed the meal down. Blackflies were biting hands and faces where sweat had erased dope. A new application silenced the menace of the North.

Lunch finished, enough to sustain them for the day ahead, the march continued. The voice of the rapids could be heard. It grew in intensity until, on a rock promontory above the pitch, they stopped in awesome silence. Below the hump of smooth water, huge rocks thrust their ugly heads and raked the raging river to shreds. A hundred yards below, it funneled into a rock-walled gorge, where it became a seething cauldron of white water, a river gone mad. Nothing could survive in the maelstrom, not even fish.

Hypnotized for a time, they pressed on toward it and the rock mass that blocked their route along the riverbank and toward civilization. Perpendicular near the water, the monument of stone sloped gradually a short distance from the river. Here, with some effort, it could be scaled. Cautiously, they picked their way. Jim used a handhold to hoist himself over the last sharp rise. Brad followed under his own power. Jim assisted the others.

Now on top, they started across the smooth rock that sloped to the river. Brad had wandered some forty yards ahead. All saw him slip, fall heavily, and slide toward the rapids a few strides away. Horror-stricken, they watched as he tried to get knees under him, then fall flat again. He clawed for a handhold, but to no avail. Legs swept over the brink, dropped; shoulders, head, he was gone. No sound was heard. Perhaps the thunderous rapids masked it.

Now out of their trance, both women, hands on their heads, screamed to the heavens. Jim moved quickly to the cliff's edge and strained his eyes for any sign in the frothing white water. Nothing could be seen. The sheer walls of the chute offered no opportunity for salvation.

Returning, he shouted, "I'm goin' down river. Don't move from this spot."

He ran across the rock and when he arrived at the place where Brad had fallen, the four left behind were astonished to see him hurdle an imaginary barrier then settle into a steady run. He dropped from view some distance below.

Petrified with grief, they huddled together like statues, not knowing what catastrophe might befall them next. Minutes dragged by, then a half hour, but still no sign of Jim. Shell-shocked from the deafening roar, they remained, afraid to take one step in any direction for fear the hungry rapids would devour them too.

Nearly an hour passed. Now they were consumed by the overwhelming dread of being left without a leader; without the man that might deliver them from this savage land.

Panic was overtaking them when Jim appeared. slowly, methodically, he came toward the four. He knew their inner feelings and could see terror in every face. It permeated their entire being. They were glad to see Jim and yet it did not register.

"Let's go!" he shouted.

All struggled up and haltingly followed to where the horrifying accident occurred. Jim signaled to stop and then yelled, "Watch where I step. Let me take your arm as you cross." Liz, hesitant and trembling, was pulled across. All made it.

There was a deep silence among them as they circumvent the gorge. Roar of the deadly rapids encompassed all.

Distance had hushed the rapids to a whisper when, finally, Jim spoke. "Let's rest here."

As they dropped the gear, John said, "Did you see anything of Brad?"

"No - we flew together many times. He was a good friend . . . a good friend."

Ellen asked, "What made him fall?"

"When we crossed the place, you may have noticed that the rock was stained and wet, where water seeped down from the ground above. Warmed by the sun, algae grew, makin' the tracing extremely slipper. Unaware, Brad stepped on it."

"Why did you let him go ahead?" John asked.

"I didn't, while I was helpin' the rest of you he wandered off, and with the roar of the river - couldn't hear his footsteps. I've seen hundreds of these traps. Possibly Brad never did, or for the moment it slipped his mind. We'll never know. Now he belongs to the river."

In quavering tones, Liz spoke. "Without Brad can we raft the river?"

"We'll be shorthanded, but it can be done."

Once more, they roused themselves but continued for less than a mile.

"We'll stay here for the night," Jim said.

"There's several more hours of daylight," Chet replied.

"Also had a trying experience. Should conserve our energy for the crossing tomorrow." He glanced at Chet. "Can you gather some spruce boughs for beddin' and a little firewood? I'm goin' downriver and check out this stretch of quiet water. Don't go back in the bush. Keep the river in sight."

With his long, effortless strides eating up the shoreline, he melted into the background. Liz sat down and attended blistered feet. Her husband sympathized with her problem, then went in search of firewood. Chet cut boughs, and Ellen helped carry them to camp. In due time, Jim returned and announced, "The river looks good for two and a half miles downstream. We're in a big back eddy that will be to our advantage. The raft can be built here where there's more timber; dead trees left high and dry from the spring breakup." Jim glanced at the water. "It's time to eat. Lake Trout should abound in this hole. Get a lure in the water while I make a fire."

Five slices of bacon sizzled in the fry pan. All devoured bacon sandwiches, Lake Trout, tea, and a bite of chocolate.

John asked, "Do you intend to cross first thing in the morning?"

Jim replied, "I'm hopin' for a little sun to warm the day and our bodies a mite before we go. We'll take the chill off round the fire anyway."

"What about the loss of Brad's equipment?" John questioned.

For the moment, Brad's demise had been forgotten, but with John's question the ghastly experienced was reflected in all of their faces. All had viewed it; all would live with it now and forever.

Finally, Jim replied, "He had some fishing tackle, medical supplies, and matches. We've got more of these items but the sleepin' bag and rope were important. I still have a hundred foot coil of nylon. Hope it's enough."

Meal finished, Jim fell to the task, gathering spruce and tamarack trunks that had lodged along the bank. The trees, bleached by weather, were more like poles, being at most five or six inches through. Chet assisted Jim, and John, more shamed into it than anything else, joined in. For some distance up and down the riverbank, they gleaned the poles. A few windfalls were added, and Jim cut some green springy trees to lash top and bottom across the raft. These would keep the others in place. Ends were notched to hold the rope that would bind them. Rough paddles and poles were fashioned for locomotion. The descending sun cast long shadows on placid water. Materials for the voyage assembled, they rested for the ordeal to come.

Jim was standing on a rock a short distance away, looking across their nemesis and beyond. Ellen watched for a moment, then approached and said, "Sometimes I look at you, staring to the distant horizon and I wonder if you are thinking that we will never get out."

Startled, he replied, "We'll get out. I can tell you not to worry but I know you will. You're not alone."

"We seem to be going so slowly."

"I try to keep one step ahead of the wilderness but you can't hurry. Learn from the river." He flicked his hand toward it. "Fall into its timeless pace and heed its every warning. Only fools don't listen." He thought for a moment of the wayward souls that remained forever in the wilderness because they tempted fate once too often.

They joined the others. Jim addressed them. "The thrust of the rapids above is toward the far shore and that means the water is movin' faster. Tomorrow we'll float the raft two hundred yards upstream on the back eddy, then out behind the shelf rock that blocks the current."

Liz interrupted. "That river scares me half to death."

"It's the greatest obstacle we'll have to face. We can beat it," Jim said.

The briefing continued. "For a while we should be able to pole the raft, but fast water or depth will leave us with only the paddle. We'll carry extra poles and paddles, but be careful. Remember, there's a rapids about two and a half miles below our startin' point - seems like a long way now, but we're not paddlin' a canoe."

Chet asked, "How fast is the current?"

"Checkin' from high ground downriver, I think it moves about five miles an hour."

John asked, "Isn't that cutting it a little fine?"

"No, I figure the river is nearly six hundred yards wide, however, that ledge rock will chop a hundred yards off it."

They bedded down and soon were sleeping the deep sleep of wanderers of the wilderness.

Dawn came too quickly, but aching bodies needed stretching and the warmth of fire to drive the cold out. Breakfast was prepared and eaten at a leisurely pace. Jim, aided by Chet and John, began building a raft on rollers near water's edge. Thin poles laid at right angles between layers made a firm foundation. Nearly finished, Jim felt the touch of a light breeze. Glancing at the water, he noted the roughened surface. The breeze was coming upriver and that was good. It would fight the current, holding them back.

The raft completed and found buoyancy under the load. Sun shone through patches of blue. Wind, steady now from the same direction. Conditions seemed right. The raft was towed to the tip of

Words of Wisdom

the rock point. They ventured forth with great apprehension on the river that had already claimed one of their number.

For a time, the men poled and made good progress. Eventually, the sweep of the current dictated a switch to the paddles.

Liz spoke, "We seem to be going downriver awfully fast."

Jim tried to calm her fears. "We're doin' okay. Keep diggin' on those paddles," he told the men.

A few minutes more brought them to mid-river; the point of no return. Jim gauged drift with headway attained. They were a mile below the launching point. Ten minutes passed; they neared shore.

"We're going to make it," cried Ellen.

"Rocks ahead," Liz shouted.

Jim answered, "I see them, but the current's slowed and it's shallow enough to pole." Let's get at it."

John was dead tired. Jim noticed his pole trailing in the water. "Get a purchase on the bottom, John. Lean on that pole."

Rocks peeked at them as they glided by. Now only thirty yards from shore, on the verge of entering a quiet eddy, the inside corner struck a submerged rock. The jolt dislodged John from the outer edge. Liz screamed. Jim looked in time to see him drop like a tree into the water. His head bobbed to the surface.

"Help me!" he shouted.

With the raft's progress all but stopped on contact, John swept past. He thrashed toward the bank.

Jim yelled, "He's holdin' his own, Chet. Let's get in. I'll run down and cut him off."

A few more pushes later, the raft was in safe water.

"Land it," Jim shouted as he jumped to hip depth, then waded to dry ground. He raced downstream and positioned himself opposite John clinging to a rock fifteen yards from the bank.

"John! There's no current inside the rock. Can you make it in?"

"I - I don't know."

The cold water had made him all but speechless and near hysteria. Jim leaped on the rock, then cleaved water. A few strokes brought him to John's side.

"We're goin' in," Jim said. Ripping John's hands from the rock, he grabbed the collar of his jacket and dragged him shoreward. They floundered to safety. Jim released his hold. John dropped to his knees. Chet, after wedging the raft between rock and shore, joined them.

"Get a fire started!" Jim spit out the words to Chet. "Somebody walk John around."

The only somebody around was Ellen. She quickly coaxed and pulled him to his feet. Liz, still seated on the raft, was giving vent to her feelings, crying uncontrollably.

John had played a deadly game. Immersed for some time, the ice cold water had taken its toll. Numbing cold had bored deep into the very core of life itself. Jim and Ellen moved him close to the fire. By convulsive efforts John removed his jacket, fighting now for self-preservation. Jim started to peel off some of his dripping clothes and Ellen, consoling Liz, led her from raft to fire. Liz hugged her husband and sat down.

Behind a rock windbreak, the fire took effect and the flickering flame of life began to rise anew in both men.

John, feeling much better, said, "I hope this is the last river we have to cross."

Jim answered, "I've flown over the area several times. There will be a few small tributaries to ford as we work our way down the Silver River, but no more raftin'. We've overcome the greatest obstacle on our journey to the coast."

"That's good news," John said.

Jim turned to Chet. "You did a good job gettin' the raft in and startin' the fire."

Their eyes met and more than words passed between them.

Rafting, to some, had been a terrifying experience, draining their resources. Jim knew they should rest.

Chet asked, "Is there anything I can do?"

Jim replied, "You can catch a few fish to take on the trip for insurance. I'll get the rope off the raft."

"Anyone want some more tea?" Ellen asked.

"That's a good point," Jim said. "I don't know if we'll find drinkin' water, so get all the fluid you can now."

All in readiness, they swung inland. Over loose stone they toiled, then followed a timeworn Caribou trail until more bare rock was reached. Slowly mounting a ridge, resting for a moment, all gazed for the last time at the angry river that would haunt them forever, then moved off over the bleak divide.

Ascending the far slope over bedrock was a relief.

Jim pointed and said, "You see those saw-tooth hills against the sky? They're about six miles away. When we reach the high ground we should see the Silver River."

The easy walking over smooth rock was of short duration. Feet cushioned by Caribou Moss soon sank into the muck of dead vegetation and the pace slowed to a crawl. They were in muskeg. Swarms of mosquitos joined ever-hungry black flies. Without insect repellant it would have been unbearable. Some still managed to inhabit eyes, ears, and noses. The ground rose slightly, their pace quickened, and the ravenous insects became fewer.

As the weary group hooked around a pond, they encountered a small laughing stream. All drank heartily, rested, and lunched on fish, tea, and bread. Ellen, seated on a stream bank, pointed to a patch of color at her feet.

"What is the name of those flowers, Jim?"

"Actually, they're called Fireweed."

She stared at them as if she would never see the beauty of flowers again. Jim plucked a few and handed them to her with a smile.

John eyed the still-distant hills that would hopefully be reached before nightfall. "Those hills look as far away as when we first sighted them."

Jim said, "We're almost halfway and the walkin' should be better."

"I can't move fast, cramps are hitting my hamstring muscles," John replied.

"We won't hurry it," said Jim.

He glanced at Liz dunking her feet at short intervals in the ice-cold brook. He was surprised she was not complaining. Rested and nourished to some extent, all drank once more and slowly joined in ragged file.

Distant hills grew in stature until the climb up the slope was begun. Pausing they looked back from whence they came. Although bone-weary from torturous terrain, there was the satisfaction of accomplishment in each of them. They struggled slowly to the summit. Two miles away gleamed again the white water of a roaring river.

John spoke, "Never thought I would enjoy seeing another river. Are you certain it's the Silver River, Jim?"

"That's it, by God! That's it!"

They moved on, following a rocky ridge that paralleled the river. A sharp descent into a saddle was achieved but the climb back up was not undertaken.

Jim said, "Time to head for the river, get something to eat, and set up camp for the night."

The downgrade was of short duration. Laboriously they slogged through the marsh, feet sliding off grassy hummocks. John, hobbled by cramped legs that would not do his bidding, twice fell headlong into the mire, but each time by virtue of his own strength he rose and tottered on. A small pothole confronted them.

Ellen spoke, "I could use a drink."

"Don't touch it," Jim said, "best to drink from runnin' water. We'll be at the river shortly."

Through small tamarack and tag alders, the bedraggled band stumbled, over rocky riverbank and down to the water's edge. They drank of water unstained by human hands, then lay back on the gravelly surface to recuperate from the exhausting march.

Jim roused himself, sought shelter, and found it in lee of a huge boulder. Shadows of the western hills were creeping along the shore. The chill of night would soon be upon them. Fire started, he put the pot to boil. The others joined him and the needed strength, all but depleted, was given bodies for the trail ahead.

Liz questioned, "How far is it now?"

"About forty miles - we'll get there." He said it with conviction. All heard, and all spirits were lifted.

Jim started off. "Gonna collect a little driftwood."

"I'll help you," Chet said.

They began to pick up sticks between rocks and throw them near the water where they could be seen on returning.

Chet spoke, "John and Liz are in bad shape. I wonder how far they can travel tomorrow."

"I realize that, but a good sleep may do wonders."

Arriving at camp they were greeted by John's pointed question. "Were you talking about Liz and me slowing you down?"

Jim did not duck the question. "We did mention it."

Liz quickly responded, "You won't leave us and send someone back?"

"Don't worry, Liz. We go together or not at all."

To some degree her anxiety was relieved.

Night closing in fast, they bedded down. A few hours later Jim stirred to the lick of chill wind on his cheek. He looked skyward. Shafts of light from the Borealis rose in the north - east to its zenith overhead, bathing the land in ghostly day. The glow outlined menacing clouds gathering to the northwest. Nature was about to play another game. Upriver, the wind was still light but determined. Spawned in the Arctic Ocean, it would in a matter of hours cause the temperature to plummet forty degrees or more. Jim fed the fire and curled up, only to repeat the process before daybreak.

They arose on legs lamed by exertion and cold, ringed the fire, and warmed their insides with tea. Mounting wind, strong from the north, had a winter's edge.

Liz spoke, "It feels cold enough to snow."

"Might before day's out," Jim replied.

"Are you serious?" John asked.

"Dead serious - icebergs east off the Labrador coast, north the Arctic Ocean, west the top of Hudson Bay. Only the south wind can warm us."

Liz questioned, "How can we stand it?"

"We have enough matches. When it gets to us we'll tuck in behind the rocks or a gully that creases the riverbank. Remember the wilderness may take something from you, but it usually gives in return. Won't be bothered by blackflies and mosquitoes."

Breakfast finished, they readied themselves for the struggle to come. Dark clouds scuttled through hills across river as they broke camp. Jim herded his charges, stopping every few hundred yards to check their progress. A mile covered, rain began to spatter on faces. Jim hooked into a gulley.

"Got to keep as dry as possible. Let's get the raingear on."

"I'm chilled to the bone," Liz sobbed.

Jim answered, "Rain gear will break the wind and keep you warmer - and I want to say one more thing. The rocks are wet now so be extremely careful. A broken leg - we're a long way from civilization." He got up and they followed.

Pelting rain became sleet. The slanting lines stung their faces. Pounded by the full flurry of the storm, with their heads bowed, strength sapped by exertion and biting cold, they fought on. Ahead, a patch of spruce on a flat above the riverbank beckoned. Jim scrambled up and assisted the others. In a slight depression among the trees, they sat on caribou moss.

Ellen questioned, "How are you feeling, Liz?"

"My legs are one big ache."

John said, "It's hard to buck the gale."

Jim said, "Our rations won't hold out forever. If we can fight our way five or six miles before day's out, we may close in on Artuk in three days."

Once more they plodded wearily along a rock-strewn shore, narrowing the distance slowly but surely against the storm and demanding wilderness. The duration of each march became shorter as Jim watched Liz and John falter. A recess in the face of the rock afforded them sanctuary from the elements. A controlled fire heated tea and orange drink. Jim placed thin strips of fish in the water that was boiling in the frying pan and took them out a few minutes later. "Cooks fast," he said, as he doled them out.

Words of Wisdom

The afternoon wore on until finally, at day's end, camp was made. Meager rations were devoured and, although exhausted, little sleep was forthcoming. Fire warmed one side while the other nearly froze. A constant rolling pervaded the seemingly endless night. Before morning, the mixture of rain and sleet ceased; the wind died to a whisper.

At first light all were ready to partake of hot tea spasmodically lifted to lips. Again, fish was eaten to slow the gnawing hunger. Bread and a piece of bacon were added.

Backs turned on another campsite. They gained a half mile, rested, and rested many times before the noon meal.

Many miles without handicap lay behind when camp was made. No hungry wind or sleet was to threaten them this night. The fire's range widened to provide greater warmth, and spent bodies were rejuvenated by deep, untroubled sleep.

Dawn came and one by one they awakened to greet a new day that seemed to foretell better things. A light southern breeze and a touch of sun were more than welcome. Breakfast without bread brought home the seriousness of the food situation. Liz asked, "How far is it to Artuk now, Jim?"

"Twenty to twenty-five miles."

"I was hoping less," said John.

"We all were," Ellen added.

John said, "The magnitude of this country awes me - the barren ground, no sign of man in all our travels."

"It horrifies me," said Liz.

Jim remarked, "We're makin' progress and we'd better make more right now."

Barely started, they encountered a large bay fringed with thick tag alders. Jim swung to high ground. A spine of rock was followed but it broke away from the river. He cut back, walked silent aisles of caribou moss amid thin spruce, then stopped to rest.

"Don't care to get far away from the river - like to hear the rapid's voice in my ear. Can't waste this time stalkin' round the bush."

Noon found them sitting on a barren bluff overlooking the river, their only route to survival. Some lay back and napped, but all too soon the trail beckoned and the assault continued.

Much daylight remained when Jim called a halt to the grueling march. Ravenously, they consumed orange drink, dehydrated soup, and the usual fish and tea.

John asked, "How are the rations?"

"We've got a packet of orange powder, one of dehydrated soup, a slice of bacon per person, a taste of chocolate, and plenty of tea."

"That won't get us far," John said.

"It should get us to Artuk even if it takes two days."

Liz remarked, "My legs are awfully weak."

Jim replied, "They'll be stronger come morning."

They met the dawn with more confidence, night's deep sleep having restored them enough to move off on a trail that never seemed to end. Two miles below, they were confronted by an obstacle that Jim had not reckoned. A branch of river barred their path.

John said, "I thought we could go all the way to the coast and not cross another river."

"I said we might have a few small tributaries to cross. I don't remember seein' this one when I flew down the river valley. It's little more than forty yards wide. Should be a spot where we can wade it."

Liz cried, "I hope so. I never want to see a raft again."

Jim said, "Rest here while I take a look."

He soon rejoined the party, waiting with great anticipation.

"How does it look?" Chet asked.

"About half a mile upstream there's a narrow lake. The walk around would be a long one even if we could cross above. Best bet is to wade a gravel bar a few hundred yards upstream."

"Any great danger?" John asked.

"There's always danger. If we're careful we can make it." Jim led them to the fording place.

"John, hold onto your wife's arm and keep as close to my path as possible. Chet, you and Ellen stay right behind. Take small steps. Be sure your foot's set before takin' another. Your legs may get numb but keep comin'."

Slowly, deliberately, Jim forged ahead. The channel in midstream was nearly three feet deep and he could feel the thrust more strongly now. Another step and the bottom angled up to the far shore. Standing in shallower water, he turned to assist them across the pocket.

"Give me your hand, Liz."

Jim pulled her over. John gained the shallows while Jim waited for Chet and Ellen inching closer to the channel. Ellen, on Chet's right, was flirting with the edge of the gravel bar. She stepped on a small rock not firmly embedded in the bottom and, like a hair trigger, it turned over. Trying to support herself, she instinctively wrenched her arm away from Chet's grasp. Dropping low in the water for a moment she floated free.

"Ellen!" Chet gasped.

Ellen struck for bottom with her other foot. It skated across gravel; her body neared buoyancy, then caught between the jaws of two rocks. Before a cry could escape her lips, she was swept under, current against her body, forcing her down. Hands protruded from the water, praying for acceptance. It was quick in coming. Chet thrashed off the bar and closed the gap. Jim fired knapsack and axe shoreward and yelled, "Grab her under the arms! Get her head up!"

He sensed what happened when drift ceased and she flagged toward bottom. Chet, finding a firm foundation, wrenched Ellen to the surface. She gasped for breath.

In anguish he shouted, "Foot's caught! Can't pull her free!"

Jim, now at their side, grabbed Chet's jacket to steady himself and said, "I'm goin' under - hold on!"

Chet mumbled, "God help her," as Jim started down.

Grasping one of the rocks holding her foot, Jim pulled - but to no avail. He placed a foot on the near face of the other rock and pried with all the strength he could muster. The rock under foot moved slightly. Jim broke surface.

"She's free!" Chet cried.

Ellen started to drift by, but Chet leaned into the current and held firm. Ellen managed to stand.

Jim hollered, "Get back to the gravel bar!"

The human chain floundered and clawed to the top, then approached the channel still before them. Jim stepped gingerly into deeper water. Facing Ellen he said, "Let me get hold of your arm. Chet, grab the collar of her jacket, and let's go."

After a few uncertain steps, they made the shallows and splashed to shore.

Jim yelled, "John, help me get some wood. Pile it by that steep bank."

Jim returned to find John trying to start some kindling. He assisted, and a roaring fire ensued.

"Get off the outer garments and move in on the fire," he said to Chet and Ellen.

Close in by the Labrador bank, the cold grudgingly gave way to the fire's warmth.

Ellen spoke, "I knew you would get me. All I could do was signal with my hands."

Chet said, "You were great. I'm shaking more from fear of losing you than from the cold."

"You will never lose me," she said, a wisp of a smile crossing her ashen face.

John asked, "How are you feeling, Jim?"

"Got the shakes but I'm all right. Let's get some tea down and have a little chocolate."

Tea on, Jim made a rack on which heavy clothing was hung. He watched it closely as it steamed from the fire's heat. Some time passed before it was thoroughly dry.

Jim said, "You had quite an ordeal, Ellen. Do you feel well enough to travel?"

"Yes, I'm ready to go."

Down the branch river they trudged to its juncture with the Silver and hopefully to civilization.

Late in the afternoon, Jim came to an abrupt halt. "I'd swear that's smoke," he said to himself. He inhaled deeply and was satisfied with his original assumption. A slight trace, but nevertheless, it was smoke - and habitation. Chet approached him. "Going to rest awhile?" he questioned.

"No - just waitin' for the others to close in."

He said nothing about the smoke. It was better not to raise false hopes for an early salvation. The north drift brought the faint scent to his nostrils once more. It was time to make camp but Jim spurred them on.

Sun was low on the western hills when Jim came upon a backbone of rock that protruded into the river, masking a sweeping bend. Gaining the height, eyes raised from the trail to the terrain ahead. He stopped short; to those behind, he beckoned with arm and word.

"We're here!"

Ellen and Chet, close on his heels, hurried to his side. They stood, awestruck, almost unbelieving, as they stared at the cabins across the river. Liz and John stumbled to join them.

Ellen, finding her voice, cried, "We made it! We made it!"

She hugged her husband as tears streamed down their cheeks. Liz and John, transfixed for a moment, followed Chet and Ellen in a warm embrace.

Jim eyed the far shore. Huskies on the riverbank started to bark. Several men scurried down the slope and soon, three freighter canoes disengaged themselves from the shoreline.

Ellen faced Jim. Rising on her toes, she kissed him and said, "Without you we would never have reached our destination - that settlement."

Jim, silent for a moment, replied, "Our destination wasn't that settlement. It was life."

Edwin Lukens

WE PROBE THE UNKNOWN

Two thousand feet below, alternate patches of water, spruce, caribou moss, and rock flashed by. Paul Martineau, a young Frenchman in the employ of Laurentian Airlines out of Schefferville near the Labrador border, was following a river valley through alternate columns of sun and rain. The sun became a less frequent visitor until finally, the lowering cloud cover shut the door and rain became a constant threat to our progress.

"I'm going to sit down for a while," Paul said.

"I won't argue with ya - let's go."

The floatplane banked steeply and retreated a few miles to a spot where the river widened and rock-free, quiet waters beckoned. Here, Paul brought the Cessna-180 down without strain and taxied to a sand-spit on a secluded bay. Anchoring the plane to some spruce trees that bordered our little beach, we pondered our predicament - but not for long. About a mile away was a rapid that we had flown over a short time before. Paul was one bush pilot that liked to fish, and the mere suggestion that we set out through the bush in a downpour, to a spot neither of us had ever fished before, didn't deter him at all. It was good to have a fellow fisherman along as crazy as I.

Ransacking the rear compartment, Paul appeared with a spinning rod and a small tackle box. Grabbing my equipment and some dope to fight the ever-present black flies and mosquitoes, we struck out through drenched spruce and caribou moss.

Nearing the river, we faced the enigma of the north - tag alders. It was a thin line, however, and we soon had battled our way through. Pausing for a moment, we surveyed the river. From the head of the rapid, looking downstream, I could not help but smile at intermittent stretches of whitewater and deep, dark pools. Some members of the finny fraternity had to reside here.

The electric chill of anticipation swept over me. Answering the call, I hopped to a rock, getting clearance from the tag alders to cast my spoon. Slightly below me, Paul had made his first cast and was starting to retrieve when his reel came to an abrupt halt, arching the pole.

"I've got one!" he yelled.

"One what?" I hollered back.

"I don't know, but dere's a big one on."

Paul had a good command of the English language, but he did supply a "d" for a "t" occasionally. Smiling at his elation. I watched the struggle. The small, wet rock where he stood was a precarious perch for such a battle. However, he somehow managed to keep his balance as the fish far out in the pool roamed from one side to the other. Slowly and skillfully, without forcing the issue, he brought the fish ever closer. Now at Paul's side, I stared into the crystal clear water for the first glimpse of the question mark on the end of his line. The monofilament angled more sharply, and soon I could see a shadowy form flagging back and forth over the rocky bottom. Then, up from the depths he came and I could see a beautiful male brook trout, resplendent in the colors of the spawning season soon to come. A few moments later, Paul held him up for my appraisal.

"A beauty - must go four pounds," I said.

"I've caught a lot of trout but never one 'dis big," he replied.

"You want to keep him?"

"I'd sure like to but I won't be going back to the base for a few days."

"No problem. The permafrost will be almost under the caribou moss and he'll keep for a long while."

"Okay, I'll set him in the tag alders."

It wasn't the last trout the pilot and I caught in the rapids. As we fished a three hundred yard stretch, we released over twenty brook trout without taking them from the water. Although we caught none bigger than the first brookie, many were in the two-to-three pound class.

I had to admit this was wonderful virgin water fishing. While surveying areas for future fishing camps and working as a guide for Laurentian-Ungava Outfitters, I had access to some of the finest fishing in the Quebec and Labrador areas. Memories of many a wild river parade through my mind's eye. The Rupert, Broadback, Whale, Kaniapiskou, Swampy Bay, Wheeler, Gue, Larch, Koksoak, and many other unknown waters visited in the past lift my spirits. Atlantic salmon and its smaller brother, the landlocked, as well as arctic char, brook, and lake trout have been caught in some number. Nevertheless, far away places, singing line, and the throbbing pole still cast their spell, so I stumble on through tag alders in search of another pool that harbors a hungry member of the finny tribe.

The brooding clouds had lifted somewhat and drenching rain had slowed to a light sifting mist chased by a slender breeze. I looked at Paul to get his reaction to the change in weather, but a hard-charging fish on the end of a taut line was holding his attention. Soon, the battle was over and a plump trout was released to swim again in friendly haunts. Over the cry of the rapid, I halted Paul.

"Weather's clearing. Let's get out of here." He nodded, and with pole in hand, skipped over a few rocks to shore. I knew he was reluctant to leave the spot, as bush pilots don't get many chances to set planes down in virgin territory to fish. From Laurentian's base in Schefferville, Paul Martineau and his compatriots fly fishermen, caribou hunters, and prospectors in and out of the bush and supply them as well. These bush pilots deserve the best. I would try to keep my companion busy on many waterways as we hopped the plane through hundreds of miles of unstained territory in search of salmon salar, the great Atlantic salmon. That was our primary objective on this trip.

Back through the bush we went. Rounding the end of a dead bay, a mother spruce partridge and four young ones were flushed. As we passed by they gawked at us from the swaying branches of a slender tamarack. Reaching the plane, we packed our fishing gear, ate a sustaining meal since it was getting late, and released our anchor ropes. With the pilot set, I lifted the tail of the plane and eased the rear of the floats off the beach. He started the engine, dropped the water rudders as I jumped on the right pontoon, and climbed aboard. Moving out to deeper water free from obstructions, we circled, warming the engine, then boomed along and in a matter of seconds were airborne.

There was still little headroom but we bored into the gloom heading northwest for a map destination that neither of us had ever seen. We crossed the mighty Kaniapiskau - a rapid below us, a maelstrom of raging white water - then over high hills as we slowly bear down on our target. The junction of the Gue and a river without name. Here we would put in a base camp and probe the surrounding wilderness by plane, canoe, and foot.

Mile after mile, we follow the nameless river sweeping the deck until there's a correlation between map and terrain. Where the Gue rushed down to join ours, the waters ran slow and deep. No doubt the ice from a multitude of breakups had scooped it out. We circled, straining our eyes for rocks that would bring us to grief, but none guarded our landing area. As we dropped lower, brooding hills that broke away from the riverbank in many places, gained dimension. Paul leveled off and gently touched her down.

"Beautiful landing. If I didn't see the spray fly from the floats I wouldn't know we were down." Paul smiled and said, "I do it all the time."

"Glad to hear that."

We taxied to the one flat area in sight - a sand beach, behind which many boulders stood like monuments in a graveyard. Hurriedly the plane was pushed back and wing tied to them. Then, axe in hand, I moved off through tag alders backed by spruce to cut poles for our small wall tent. Extra poles provided stakes which in turn were rocked down to prevent a fast-rising wind from ripping the tent out by the roots and taking it to a quieter spot. This accomplished, rubber mats were placed and sleeping bags added along with supplies that needed cover. Night was falling fast, and after a rather harrowing day, coaxing to sleep wasn't necessary. Into the bags we went, with dreams of catching fish where no man had tried before.

Up early, we cook the old standby bacon and eggs, and with cleanup behind us, eagerly pack lunch and gear, then load the faithful plane. If weather permits, a square-tail canoe and fuel for our outboard will be delivered by twin Beechcraft today. But for two days the plane will stay with me, and so we will range far from base, checking lakes and rivers previously marked on the map.

We're off the water, heading downriver in a strong wind but no rain. Sun, a not-too-frequent visitor, fingers through a thin cloud cover. When you want to wet a line, the flying seems to take an eternity. The first area designated on the map is not to our liking. I held the map for Paul's appraisal. "I guess we can cross that spot off," I said. Paul nodded, then added, "We might get down alive but the plane wouldn't live it out."

Staring out the side window as we whipped by, I reaffirmed his logic. The water ran fast, but the main problem was a bumper crop of rocks that reared their ugly heads above and just below the surface. A short distance beyond, the river widened and its dark water gave some satisfaction so we scanned it at a lower altitude. Satisfied that no hazards lay in wait, we landed and tied down the plane. All fishermen expect action every time they cast and I was somewhat stunned because nothing struck while we pounded the water for a mile or more upriver. Spirits drooping, we wandered back, hoping the next spot would prove more fruitful.

In the air once more, we flew inland away from our river valley. Over ridges, lakes, and streams the little 180 carried us. Breasting a rocky plateau we caught the gleam of white water far out on the distant horizon. Our second fishing area would soon be under us. Another river without name, only a line on a map, yet flowing mile upon mile until its crystal clear waters eventually mingled with salt. Below the rapid, soapsuds sweep this way and that way on the tracings of boils from rocks far down in the depths. It afforded us a safe landing and after the administering to the needs of the plane, we hurriedly converge on the tumbling water above.

From the base, we can see several beautiful pools between rims of whitewater. Ideal spots for brook trout, ouananiche, even lake trout might be at home here. Another thought comes to mind. Perhaps the aristocrat of all fish, the Atlantic salmon haunts the river. I mull it over for a moment but drop it when I think of the distance to the coast and who knows how many obstacles in between. One good falls and that's the end of the run.

Paul sprinted ahead with intentions of getting a line wet as soon as possible. Now out of sight behind a rocky point, I hear his shout over the song of white water. "Dere here!"

I stumbled quickly around the rocky ledge to see my companion, feet dug in gravel, hanging onto a bowed rod. My mind was geared for salmon. I sighted down the taut line straining eyes for a glimpse of a fish with a flight plan. The surface remained unbroken.

"It must be a trout," I said.

"I don't know what it is but it's givin' me a good fight."

A throbbing pole and line cutting water over an expansive pool testified to that. "Bring it in so I can see it," I chided. "I'm tryin'," he said sternly, and then smiled as he realized I was giving him a friendly needle. Standing near, I watched the fight until a few minutes later, close in, across the bright gravel bottom came a king-sized speck. "It's a beauty, Paul. Goin' to keep him?"

"No, I'll let him go."

He squatted at the water's edge and although the trout spooked a few times it ended in Paul's hands and was quickly released. Slowly waving goodbye with a large straight tail, it headed for the confines of a friendly hole. It was doubtful that anyone would ever again have the thrill of catching this lunker square tail.

Still thinking of this possibility, I was aroused from my reverie once again by Paul who seemed to enjoy piloting fish as much as planes.

"I've got another one."

And so he had. I looked up just in time to see a small ouananiche, or landlocked salmon, as it is commonly known, angle clear of the surface and with thrashing tail skitter a few feet before disappearing from view. It cut a few more holes in the water but because of its size was at my companion's feet in short order. Being close at hand I thought I'd help Paul by releasing the little fellow. Grasping him carefully I looked him over. I was stunned by what I saw. The fish was not a landlocked, but a small Atlantic salmon. A parr, to be exact. We were definitely on a salmon river. Sometime during the summer, a run or two would pass this spot.

With the catching of the parr, fly fishing was dictated. I had been using spinning tackle most of the time, as had Paul. It might well be that no man had ever fished here let alone caught a salmon in this isolated place hundreds of miles from the nearest base. However, we had fly rods in the plane and we were soon whipping the water. After several hours of searching, some decent trout and a few more parr had come our way but no large salmon. Our high hopes dashed, we disconsolately picked our way back to the waiting Cessna and winged down through the hills until we were once again at our base camp.

I was unhappy enough over the salmon fishing but when I scanned the beach and found no canoe in evidence, I was more disappointed. Evidently the weather had socked in the Beechcraft. Of course it might be in tomorrow - although nothing could be counted on in this country. The weather changes from one mountain or river valley to the next and we were far away from the main base.

The sun had fallen behind a mountain of rock on the far side of the river, and night would soon be on us. A warm meal was stowed away and dishes washed. Then we moved toward warm sleeping bags, as the night was cold as most nights are near the north coast of Canada. Besides we needed to rest our bones for another long day of travel. A determined wind rattled the tent but we paid little heed and soon were sleeping the deep untroubled sleep of the wanderer.

Another day came and moved swiftly by as we checked more unknown territory without finding a salmon. We were more than a little subdued as we poured over the problem at suppertime and then turned in.

I awoke to a day dawning with all the brilliance of a coalmine at midnight. A bitter wind moving upriver chilled me to the core as I staggered down to the water's edge to wash. Paul joined me in shivering and also in coffee, bacon, and eggs. Thus fortified, we planned the day's schedule. Paul would be heading back to the base by late afternoon and as he had little reserve gas our only alternative as to work the river around camp.

Our gear collected, we checked to see that the plane was anchored securely and then started our hike upriver. We hadn't gone far when a large family of Canada geese ran hurriedly from bush to water. The adults honked the little ones along.

About a half mile above camp, the river made a sharp bend and moved in a glassy glide. Here, sheltered to some degree from the wind, we could work a fly with some proficiency and hopefully keep it from ripping into an ear.

I stopped near the base of the glide, perhaps because the current, depth of water, and gravel bottom closely resembled other stretches of river where salmon had come to my fly. I set my pack down, started to put my fly rod together, and addressed Paul. "I'm going to work here for a while."

"I'll go up by dat boulder," he said.

By the time I positioned myself to work the line, Paul had disappeared behind the huge boulder some distance above. My cast was made with the same anticipation of a thousand other first casts but no monster rushed to devour my offering. Time and again I fanned the water close in, but to no avail.

I began to reach out. Then, as the fly swept down and started to cut an arc toward shore, my pulse quickened as the fly stopped short. Instinctively, I struck back and almost instantaneously the water parted and a large streamlined missile rose straight up, clearing the surface by at least two feet. He succumbed to the force of gravity and fell back with a resounding splash. I held the rod high, a little late, but we were still connected by line and straining five-pound leader. The tug of war would continue, at least for a few seconds.

A dark thought crossed my mind. As the leader was not new, I couldn't be certain of its strength. Caution would prevail but with a salmon approaching fifteen pounds on the end of the line, he would have much to say about the eventual outcome. A short run, another great leap, and I was at the end of my fly line. A hundred yards of monofilament backing began to roll off the reel. Straight out into the river he ended a run with another jump. Then the silver torpedo angled downstream, tearing off the line with reckless abandon until, finally turning back toward shore, I was able to pick up a little slack. Backing almost gone, I prayed he wouldn't run again. If he did, there would be nothing I could do except wait for the leader to part. But luck was still in my corner. His mad rushes were confined to the big back eddy below primarily caused by the bend in the river. Several more times he jumped and although he gained a slack line on numerous occasions somehow he remained hooked. Walking slowly along shore picking up line, I reached a point opposite the fish.

All the pressure I dared was put to bear in hope of keeping my friend in quiet water and possibly move him shoreward. He made several short rushes without jumping until finally he was almost motionless beside the rock I was perched upon. He shied as I reached down to tail him. Just a few slips of a powerful tail and then I had a grip on the beautiful Atlantic.

Battle over, I brought him to shore and up the steep bank to a patch of caribou moss between tag alders. I would keep this one to take back to the base and of course have a surprise for Paul who was still out of sight upriver. Covering the fish with a few tag alder branches, I turned again toward the river. On a rock a short distance above my last spot, casting was resumed and I was soon fast to another salmon of lesser size but none the less a worthy adversary. I gloried in his fight for freedom and when the battle was over I reached down and gently released him, hoping another fisherman would one day feel through the electricity of pole and line the driving runs and delight in his powerful leaps. Maybe the odds were against it, but if the area proved to be a good one, a camp might be erected in the near future and others would come to pay homage to the mighty salmon.

Fishing was continued and so engrossed was I that I didn't notice Paul until he was close at hand. I turned to see him smiling broadly, and for good reason. He was dragging a salmon with his right hand that was at least as large as mine. "Where did ya get him?"

"About a hundred yards above the big boulder. Caught him on this gray ghost streamer. Thought I might catch a large brook trout. It may not be an accepted salmon fly but it sure works."

Casting an envious eye I replied, "I'll say it works. That's a beaut." I had to show him my fish so I stumbled up the bank and held it up for his approval. We left the two salmon bedded down under caribou moss and continued on our way. Luck accompanied us. As the day wore on, several more Atlantics came our way. Such fishing is extremely hard to turn one's back on but the time had come for us to return to camp and part company. Paul had some duties to perform back at the base for the next four days. I would remain, and if no canoe arrived, take long forays up and down river on foot to complete our survey of the area.

We arrived at the tent carrying two salmon and still swapping details of the days' fishing. Quickly we packed the plane with Paul's equipment and put the fish aboard. Anchor lines were untied. I bucked the tail of the 180 and pushed it out into the current, then shouted, "Have a good trip. See ya in four days if the weather's good." He waved from the open door and then snapped it shut. The idling engine mounted to greater life as he taxied out to deeper water. After warming awhile, Paul throttled it up and in a shower of spray, jumped of the river. In a matter of seconds the little plane had swung the bend above camp and disappeared behind a mountain of rock.

The noise of the engine still reverberated from the rocky crags that walled my river as I shuffled tent-wards to prepare an early supper. I thought of days spent searching countless river valleys by plane and on foot, only to find the silvery salmon within a half mile of base camp. While the plane was with us, we relied on it heavily, figuring when it left I could range eight to ten miles up and down river on foot, if necessary.

Only because the gas supply was low did Paul get his chance to connect with the king of fish. I was happy for him and also the others that might one day enjoy the fishing we had experienced on an unknown river near the north coast of Canada.

TED WILLIAMS - I KNEW HIM WHEN

With Ted Williams' passing, many of his exploits come to mind. He hit 400 and also had a tremendous record amassing home runs and runs batted in during a long career. He was probably the greatest hitter of all time, and might have broken Babe Ruth's home run record, but for two tours of duty as a Marine pilot in World War II and Korea.

Almost five years were taken from him and it is amazing that on returning to the game he played so well. No doubt it was a fight to get in shape again. He was a true hero, having answered his country's call. I believe in Korea he was wingman for John Glenn.

I was never one to collect autographs, but I certainly have deep admiration for Ted. While guiding in upper Quebec and Labrador, Ted came into camp. At the time, a sportsman's program involving fishing was running on TV on Sunday afternoons during the winter months. A corps of reporters and photographers would accompany a few celebrities as they fished.

Ted alighted from the floatplane and stepped on the floating spruce dock. He noticed me coming out to assist the operation and evidently, thinking I was a guide, asked the leading question "What they hittin' on?" Most fishermen would probably use the term "biting" or "taking," but being a hitter, that was fitting for Ted. I may have told him at the time that a clothespin would do, and more seriously a Muddler Minnow was good, but many flies would work on Atlantic salmon here.

I found out that Ted reached out much farther than a fish pole. The environment concerned him to a great extent. He told me of the devastation wrought by DDT in the Maritime Provinces. He said the bird life was decimated and the Osprey was almost wiped out. Ted was a fine fly fisherman and had a cabin on the Miramichi River in New Brunswick and saw first-hand the ravages of DDT.

Ted was also involved in charity work, primarily the Jimmy Fund, to which he contributed heavily. I wasn't with Ted for long, but

I enjoyed his company. He was a likeable guy with a ready smile and he was at peace with the world.

Well, Ted, I hope there's a baseball diamond in heaven and you hit a few home runs for the Lord's team. God bless you, Ted.

A LAUGHING MATTER

The sky was gray with the threat of rain as I headed for the roadside mailbox. Wind from the Northwest, although light, had a cutting edge that whispered of winter's song. I heard the haunting call of Canadian geese and far out on the horizon, a ragged arrowhead mounted the Northern sky. As they passed overhead I was distracted from my gaze by Gotch's battered blue pickup turning into my drive. He dismounted and said, "Saw ya standin' there like a statue with your mouth open lookin' skyward. Thought ya might be havin' an attack or something and need assistance."

"No, just watching the honkers and wishing I could head south, too."

Gotch lowered the tailgate on the truck.

"Back hurts when I stand too long." He hoisted his spare frame to a sitting position and added, "Join me."

As I did so I smiled and said, "I've got a lot of work to do. You don't intend to settle down and make this somewhat permanent, do you?"

He laughed. "No, haven't seen ya in some time, thought we'd jaw for a little while."

"I see you've got a few boxes of groceries," I said.

"Yeah, been to town. None of it will spoil though, so quit tryin' to get rid of me. Ya know, the prices are like next year. Almost had to hock the truck to pay for 'em. Got a cheap cut of meat, if ya can call it that. Figure it saved me a little and chewin' it for several days gives me a lot of good exercise. Last week the hardware store had an ad in the Pennysaver. Some of the articles marked down I've been hankerin' to get so I went on a little spree. Ya know how they say save two dollars on this article and five on another? Well I saved twelve dollars but when I walked out of the store I found $38 missing from my pocket."

"Yes, I've done that too," I said.

"Did ya ever notice how everything is 'only' or 'just'?"

"What do ya mean by that?"

"Well, you see in the paper where a beautiful Colonial home sells for 'only' $62,000 or a Cadillac is 'just' $14,000, as if they were paltry sums."

"You're right. I also wonder about bargain sales. One store sells everything for a 25% discount. Last week they probably jumped the price 25%."

"Ya know," Gotch said, "Henty had a salesman stop at his farm the other day and try to sell him a snow blower. Henty said he had a tractor that took care of most of the snow removal. The salesman pointed to a machine in his catalog and replied, 'This snow blower will take care of the small jobs that you can't use the tractor on. It will toss snow 240 degrees.' Henty wasn't much impressed. He said he had a snow thrower that tossed it 360 degrees. The salesman said he had never heard of such a machine."

"What kind is it?"

"Henty replied, 'A four and a half foot shovel.' Ya know, one of the greatest weapons to go the distance is a sense of humor, and that Henty's sure got one. He's one corn crop away from seventy-two and still doin' the same chores he always did; maybe slowin' down a mite but he gets the work done."

I said, "Not long ago, I told him he ought to get some help and take it easy. I don't know as I fully comprehended his answer, but there was some food for thought. He said, 'Ya got to look at it this way. There's no time to relax if ya do nothin'.'"

Gotch said, "One day he told me his dentures kept fallin' out but he thought the problem was solved now. 'Used some a that super glue,' he said. 'I've got a hunch they're gonna stay with me to the grave and maybe for some time thereafter.' The mention of grave seemed to put him in a pensive mood and I thought he was goin' to be serious for a moment. Finally he spoke. 'Ya know, I've lead a good life. When my time comes I sure hope the Lord will let me through those pearly gates. I was a pretty good churchgoer. Sometimes I went twice on Sunday; dropped the wife off and picked her up later.'"

I got laughing so hard the truck was going up and down.

Gotch said, "That Henty's a beaut. Well, I got to be goin'." He jumped off the tailgate. I followed suit. As I waved goodbye I thought to myself, "That makes two beauts."

UNDERSTANDING AN OGRE
(ALTERNATE TITLE: THE OTHER SIDE OF THE COIN)

I was 7 years old when Mr. and Mrs. Denby and their 5 year old daughter, Ann, moved in next door. They had only lived in this country a few years, having come from England. Mrs. Denby was an outgoing woman and she and mother soon became good friends. Mr. Denby seemed to be the direct opposite of his wife: quiet, non-smiling, and highly protective of his solitude. In fact, he became known as somewhat of an ogre on Landmark Avenue. His late-night walks also aroused the neighbors' curiosity.

In the late 1920s there were many youngsters in the neighborhood and the majority were about my age. If we made a racket near Mr. Denby's house and he was there we were immediately told to move away. It did not set well with the kids because many times we were not on his property but in the street. We carried out his bidding, although on occasion a few heated words were exchanged.

Mr. Denby was not an imposing figure. He was rather short, thin, but sinewy, with dark hair and a swarthy complexion. Actually, he was quite a handsome man.

As the years went by, even a youngster like me could not help but notice that beneath the rough exterior we kids knew there dwelled a different man - a devoted family man - patient, kind, and diligent in his care of house and yard. Rarely did he miss a day on the job as a printer on the evening newspaper.

One hot Fourth of July, I thought Mr. Denby was going to kill some of the kids on the block. At that time the Fourth was celebrated with everything short of dynamite. As the first early salutes shattered the serenity of our street I heard the windows close in Mr. Denby's house. I did not see Mr. Denby in the morning, but on occasion Mrs. Denby requested the boys setting off their firecrackers, cherry bombs, and aerial bombs to keep away from the house.

In the afternoon, however, Mr. Denby sallied forth and screamed like a crazy man at all who ventured near. Finally, in desperation to escape the din, he walked up the street with his dog, Patch, into the more peaceful surroundings of the reservoir grounds and countryside above his home.

A few days after the Fourth of July celebration, father and I were in the backyard one early evening, throwing a baseball. Mother was tending her garden when Mrs. Denby and her daughter came over to visit.

Later, Mr. Denby joined us and while the women talked, Mr. Denby invited father and I for a drink. The invitation was surprising, as it was the first in the five years he had lived there. The refreshments consisted of coffee for the grownups and a soda for me.

Mr. Denby was uneasy and found it difficult to speak. Finally, he looked across the kitchen table at my father and stammered, "I must apologize for my actions the other day. You see, I cannot stand noise."

Then, as if the floodgates opened, years of pent-up feelings gushed forth in his words.

"In the war I served with the British forces in France. After two years in the trenches under the almost continuous pounding of artillery, my nerves were shot. Then, in a German offensive, we were cut off and captured.

"The next year and a half was spent in a prisoner of war camp. The treatment there did not help the situation. I nearly starved to death. Many of the men interned with me died of starvation or disease brought on by lack of nutrition. My weight dropped from 146 pounds on entering service to 84 pounds at war's end."

I listened intently to every word as Mr. Denby continued.

"On occasion a doctor would come in but did little to alleviate the suffering. Many times he greeted me in broken English with, 'You not dead yet?' The last day in the camp was the worst one. I was too weak to climb on the truck. Two Germans grabbed me, arms and legs, and threw me on like a sack of grain. Being nothing but a bag of bones when I landed, it almost killed me."

He hesitated a moment, then added, "That is why I went on a tirade the other day - the firecrackers - I do not like to be reminded of war. I'm sorry."

"No need to be," my father said.

Now I had a better understanding of the man some called an ogre.

JUST A DOG

Now and then in passing, one hears the term "fur person." In my youth, we had a "fur person" by the name of Ginger. He was a large, curly-haired Airedale. When he was in the house I don't believe anyone ever arrived at the front door without being announced. Four wooden steps had to be mounted and the first tread on them evoked a bark; just one, and all knew we had a visitor.

A half-mile from our house was a park area where we played baseball. From a grassy bank near third base, Ginger viewed, and seemingly laughed at, our ineptitude. Occasionally when a grounder came down the third base line, he'd dash on the diamond and help the third baseman make the play. Ginger could make unerring catches with his mouth but his throw to first was weak. I really don't think he had his heart in baseball because he never went to second for the double play.

Trout fishing was more in Ginger's line, probably because of his love for water. Lying beside me on the bank, he cocked an ear to the voices of nature and barked at struggling fish on the end of my line. Sometimes he chose a closer vantage point, standing in the stream and giving advice. I thought he might help land the trout, but I don't think he cared for the smell of fish. When I tossed one on the bank, he would tickle it with his paw, but never mouth it.

Occasionally, on a hot day, he took to the water, lying in the stream, little more than his head out, the water washing over him. This maneuver wasn't conducive to my catching fish, however. Somehow I had the feeling Ginger was wondering why I was sitting in the hot sun when I could be enjoying the cool refreshing water.

Many of the most eventful trips were to Pogey Pond. Actually, it was an old reservoir over two miles from home. We cut across fields and woodlands into the heart of nature. Ginger constantly nosed back and forth in the grass and brush in front of me. Many a surprised rabbit, squirrel, or chipmunk was put to run.

At times I watched as he treed a squirrel. Gaining sanctuary on a limb well above Ginger, the squirrel often lay there scolding, tail pulsating with each utterance. Forepaws on the tree, Ginger shouted right back to show the squirrel who was boss.

Of the multitudes of animals that scurried before his charges, none was ever caught - not that it wasn't possible. His mad dashes were of short duration. Possibly he acted in this manner thinking he was protecting me from all enemies lurking along the way.

One of Ginger's most comical stunts was first viewed at Pogey Pond. While I was sitting on the bank and fishing, I noticed Ginger stalking some unsuspecting creature along the nearby shoreline. He stopped, raised his right front leg, and slowly brought it down. Suddenly, a frog leaped out and plopped into the water. When this happened Ginger's front end collapsed; forelegs straight out, he gave strong voice to punctuate the action. This procedure was continued along water's edge on either side of me. Actually, I could see he had no intention of catching the frogs. In fact it was more like a tickle just to see them jump and splash into the water.

Ginger enjoyed swimming even in winter's snows, but start to gather a few essentials to administer a bath, and a decided change took place in his attitude. If I uncoiled the hose in the heat of summer, the sinister act was fully noted. He would slink away and the chase began. In one of the cold months I had Ginger trapped in the cellar and started to draw water in one of the big double washtubs. Knowing disaster was about to descend, he retreated in fast order up the cellar stairs. The door looked shut but the latch hadn't fallen into position. Ginger nosed it open and quickly found a hiding place. I ransacked the house, looking under beds, checking closets, until finally I peered over my father's lounge chair in one corner of the living room. The narrow opening between wall and chair was just wide enough for Ginger to squeeze through and there he lay, still as death.

In the living room to the right of the chair where I usually sat was a throw rug that Ginger took as his own. Lying close to me meant Ginger got scratched behind the ears regularly. From time to time he would bring his head back, twisting it to the left, and roll his eyes up like someone peering over the rims of eyeglasses. This was his way of saying things were all too quiet and we had better get some life into the act.

If I said to Ginger, "Let's go out," his tail wound up like a self-starter until it wagged the whole dog. Away from the confines of the house, he pranced back and forth, then returned to place his paws on my chest or jump so that his head was aligned with mine. He seemed to be saying, 'we're going to have a good time today.' His enthusiasm infected me - a joy of surroundings undiminished. When we set out, it was always with anticipation, for our sojourns afield were always eventful. He was a fine teacher and the truest of friends, constant in his affection. If the events of the day were depressing, I could turn to him to change my mood. We grew dependent on each other. Also, I had the strange feeling that I wasn't watching over him as he was watching over me.

It was regrettable when the span of years is so short that a dog passes from puppyhood to a time when he can only acknowledge your presence with a lift of head or wag of tail.

In the spring of his 11th year, Ginger passed from my life. It was a long time ago. I was deeply saddened then . . . I am saddened now.

OUT OF THE DARKNESS

I was about seven years old when, due to my mother's illness, I became part of my grandparents' household. There I resided for over two years and, but for one person, it would have been a disaster. My grandmother and grandfather were fine people; however, it might have been quite an imposition to take me into their home. My grandmother had lost her first husband when my mother, sister, and brother were very young. He had died of gangrene from a burst appendix, leaving her with the upbringing of the grandchildren. She was soon joined by my great-great-aunt, whose name was Rosa, but soon became known as Rosie.

I arrived in troubled times. The stock market crash of '29 had just taken place and grandfather was trying to hold onto his job. Being seven years old I had no comprehension of the problems at hand. The routine was always the same, with little caring or happiness prevalent. I was not ill-treated but gloom seemed to persist day after day. Perhaps I thought it was due to my presence. Around my former home were many children about my age so I had several friends. Now I had no friends and little possibility of finding any, as the area was devoid of youngsters.

The loss of friends and my dog, and the lack of warmth and understanding from others had taken a toll. To reiterate, my grandparents gave me a home that encompassed a comfortable bed and good meals. However, there were times I thought of leaving when darkness seemed overwhelming.

It was then that a pixie came into my life. This was my great-great-aunt, Rosie. Evidently, for a while she had been sizing up the situation. Maybe she thought entering my life was not for a person of her years, or that I might find someone in the neighborhood about my age. Becoming cognizant of the fact that my world was limited with no avenue to raise my spirits, she jumped wholeheartedly into the fray. Diminutive, bowed, with an abundant crown of snow-white hair, Aunt Rosie was a God-given link that kept me on an even keel. We all have problems, and I have had more than a few, but in one of the darkest periods of my life Aunt Rosie became the rock against the storm. She brought me out of the depths of despond.

We set out on safaris. That was her term for the many forays into the fields to pick daisies or to see tadpoles and frogs in the swamp beyond. We climbed the south bank of the Woodland Reservoir where we could view seagulls, ducks, killdeer, snipe, and even fish. She was over 80 at the time but still moved as if she had denied the advance of years. Of all our endeavors, I think her greatest satisfaction and happiness was found in our sojourns through fields and woodlands. Without a doubt she delighted in the flowers, butterflies, bird life, and all the Lord's creatures.

Her days had been filled with sewing, knitting, making quilts, housework, and cooking, but still she found time for me. In my mind's eye I can see her with head slightly bowed, eyes a-twinkle, peering over gold-rimmed glasses. I hear her say, "Eddie, what will we do next?" Aunt Rosie could always answer that question.

It was long ago that Aunt Rosie came into my life, yet to this day she has a strong hold on my memory. No one in my lifetime was as caring and kind as that grand little lady.

I have a hunch that she is keeping house for the Lord and probably doing the cooking too. You sure are lucky, Lord.

LIFE IN THE WOODCUTTER'S UNION

Gotch, Mosey, and I were cutting beech for firewood in Gotch's lot when it came time for lunch. The respite was welcome in more ways than one. You don't talk much when chainsaws are chewing away and it isn't difficult to understand what noise pollution means either.

Our cafeteria consisted of two logs. For a while not a word passed between us, so intent were we on getting some fuel down the hatch. Gotch, having quelled his hunger to some degree, was first to speak. "Mosey, if ya keep runnin' that chain with reckless abandon you're gonna end up in the marble orchard."

"Not me, but if I ever do cash in I'll phone ya when I reach my destination."

Gotch replied, "Where you're goin' the phone would melt."

"More friends like you I don't need," said Mosey. "Come to think of it, if heaven is my reward it will be nice to see my best friend again . . . my dog."

"Mosey," I said, "to get back to wood, it seems to take a tremendous amount to heat that house of yours."

"And with good reason," he replied. "The old house is not only big but it doesn't have any insulation. One day last winter, I was eatin' supper and we had a quick change of weather. A south wind was roaring through cracks around the back door. Quick as a bunny that just sat in some of my wife's chili pepper sauce, a north wind whirled through cracks around the front door. They met in the dining room and it snowed on my rhubarb pie, and rhubarb pie a la mode ain't none too good."

I said, "The location of the house doesn't help either, situated as it is on a hill where it catches the wind."

Mosey said, "On cold nights before my wife can get the food from stove to table it's usually frozen."

"You know," Gotch said, "with us feedin' our faces and talkin' about food I just happened to think of a statement Clem made the other day. He said, 'I see these commercials now where the food is finger-lickin' good, but with my wife's cookin' you don't do that...once around is enough.'"

I laughed and said, "I guess her cookin' isn't the greatest but he'll never starve to death. He usually has some game in the freezer and a load of fish."

Mosey said, "He's a good fisherman. Some time ago I asked him if he was goin' to be on the stream for the rainbow run come spring. He replied, 'Lately that may be the problem; gettin' too old I guess. I can't run with them anymore. I'd do much better if they walked.'"

Mosey picked up a bottle and took a healthy swig. As he set it down, Gotch said, "What's in the bottle, whiskey?"

Mosey replied, "You knotheads know I don't drink. This is tea."

Gotch said, "Don't ya ever get tempted to take a drink of the hard stuff?"

"A little, I suppose," Mosey answered. "But I keep away from it. However, there are other things that tempt me and I give in now and then. Don't want to take them too lightly. I figure some may never come again."

Gotch said, "Talkin' about temptation, you know that parcel of land that Sam Jackson was thinkin' of sellin'? Clem had his eye on it for some time, mainly because it bordered his property. A few weeks ago someone approached Sam and offered him $20,000 for it. The guy said he was going to put up a house and wanted the extra acreage to raise horses. Sam figured $20,000 was a pretty good price so he told the guy okay. A few days later the fellow came back and said he couldn't come up with the money right away but he would shortly. Sam told Clem about it and Clem said at that rate he could offer $30,000."

Mosey laughed and said, "It's mighty easy to buy things when ya don't have to come up with the money." He placed a sandwich bag in his lunch basket and added, "Men, I think if we're gonna get any wood out of this lot we'd better get at it. Anyhow, the way Gotch is talkin', he may get an ulcer not knowin' when he's through."

A FRIEND IS A FRIEND, IS A ...

We met - James Cleary and I - at such an early age that I have no recollection of the moment, but I am well aware of the long and enjoyable friendship that followed, for they enhanced my life.

The multi-faceted paths of youth left traces on my mind. Perhaps the passing years make them brighter. Certainly they enriched my days as the thought does now. In retrospect, I can assess those moments of companionship and place a far greater value on them, than my boyish mind could comprehend.

In youth, our gods dwelled in the fields and woodlands and to an even greater degree in athletic endeavors. We played football, baseball, hockey; later, tennis and golf. In hockey, there seems to be a tendency toward mayhem, usually cropping up after the poke of a stick handle to the ribs or stinging swat of blade to the shins. Yet, in all our competitive combat, Jim never involved himself in extra-curricular activities or even heated arguments - discussions, yes, but his concentration was on winning the game, not the deviate skirmishes. He held true to this pattern in the years ahead - not having any ability for defeat, he channeled his energies toward goals. His main goal was to become a surgeon, and he traveled the long hard road to a successful conclusion. He tested his will many times. For some years, smoking was a daily ritual. Then, suddenly, the cigarette was missing and I asked, "Why?" He said, "Studies have been published lately that paint a black picture and I've got to think of my family." Once he made a commitment there was no doubt as to the outcome.

I remember well a time in our late teens when four of us gathered to play cards. Our hosts' parents were away, so the duration of the game was unrestricted. Most of the Friday or Saturday night games broke up around midnight.

The room where we played was devoid of a timepiece, nor was there a watch among us. Eventually, our close concentration on every turn of the cards began to wane, heads started to nod, and the game broke up On the front porch, Jim and I paused in amazement. We could not understand why it was so light without a full moon. Then, a robin sang from a giant poplar tree in the side yard. As the day dawned, so did the truth. Jim exploded in a gale of laughter.

With Jim there was no pretense. He never did acquire a polite, put-on laugh. In ecstasy he thrashed around, his ample 6-foot, 1-inch frame bumping me in the process. His infectious laughter permeated my whole being and we roared in unison. So weak did we become that we had to sit down on the top porch step to regain our composure.

I believe it was at the time of Jim's internship that he phoned me more than once to say, "Let's take in a movie."

When I arrived at the back door, Mrs. Cleary - most of the time tidying up the kitchen - would tell me Jim was in the living room. As a rule, I found him sound asleep in an easy chair with a newspaper across his lap. Knowing he was exceptionally tired and needed sleep more than anything else, I visited with his parents for a while and then returned home. Soon, Jim would phone and rebuke me in mild manner for not waking him. I knew it too, as an apology, Jim thinking my evening had gone awry.

In later years, after Jim had become a surgeon but was still living in the neighborhood, I was the first to arrive at his house one evening for a get-together. HIs father had come down with some minor affliction and I questioned Jim about his present condition. He answered that he was fine and then asked me if I was healthy.

"I'm always okay," I replied smiling.
I could see a diabolical glint in his brown eyes as he said, "I can remedy that. Come out in the kitchen. You need a shot."

"Shot for what?"

"Polio."

"Don't the kids need those shots?"

"We've covered the kids. You old duffers need them now."

The shot given, I made the mistake of trying to pay for it I received another shot - a rabbit punch to the ribs and the comment, "You will pay for it in more ways than one if I ever get you on the operating table."

If I was saddened by some happening in the day's events, it became a challenge for Jim to lift my spirits. I suppose that is one of the mainsprings of friendship. When tragedy struck - the loss of loved ones - he did not intrude beyond the expression of sympathy, but his presence was an acknowledgement of support and it eased the hurt. At my father's death he traveled over 200 miles from his present home to be with me.

I did not notify him of my father's passing because of the demands of his profession; not because it was a private affair. He was part of the family anyway. I never knew who relayed the message to him, but I do know as a few relations gathered, he came through the door and no one was more welcome. For his acts of kindness, I do not think it possible to balance the ledger in my lifetime.

Jim faced himself as well as any man I ever knew, and he acquired a depth of understanding and inner serenity brought about by a thirst for life and the challenge of his profession; a profession that leaned hard on mind and body. Overall, his bedside manner and sense of humor lasted the years.

Barring an emergency, Jim was in church early Sunday morning. Although not of penitential fervor, he was a genuinely religious man - a keeper of the flame. His religion was not a one-day ritual. In the ensuing period between Sundays, he kept and practiced the covenants of brotherhood.

One Sunday morning, after returning from church and the usual visitation with his patients, I noticed he was downcast. As we sat in the backyard, sitting opposite each other at a picnic table, he told me of the patient he had lost. It did not matter that the man was over 80 years old or that he would die if the operation was not performed. He had lost a patient.

I often think some of his competitiveness came from athletics; regardless, it is in his makeup. He has performed thousands of operations but the theme never changes. Death peers over his shoulder and Jim does all in his power to drive him back into the shadows.

The sun was low on the western hills as I drove the winding road to Jim's home one evening in the heart of summer. Just short of his driveway, I came upon Jim with his youngest son in tow. I parked the car and greeted him. The tails of his sweat-stained shirt hung down, covering the top of his baggy, dirty-kneed pants. Evidently, he had been working in the vegetable garden shortly before. He looked more like a tramp than a prominent surgeon and I chided him about it.

He replied, "My neighbors tolerate me. I haven't been picked up for vagrancy yet."

Keeping up with the Joneses or putting on airs was not his style. What did matter was character. The pages of Jim Cleary's life are open for display. No shame is written there. His honesty and moral integrity are still intact, locked behind a flashing Irish grin that greets one and all.

Weekends spent with the doctor were frequently interrupted. In the earliest of hours on Sunday morning, he labored over four teenagers whose car had crashed into a tree. Near dawn he arrived home, only to receive another emergency call that sent him back to the hospital. Such demands on his services were not unusual. I know too of the many operations performed for those in need without recompense.

Although we suffered major disruptions of companionship - World War II and opportunities of profession that took Jim to new localities - our friendship has only strengthened by experience shared over the years. Out of the multitudes we were brought together and I am thankful for having known this man.

A MAN OF THE SOIL RETURNS

As I walked the road that skirted the western edge of the cemetery, I noticed a solitary figure standing on the hillside among the markers. On closer inspection, I saw it was Henty. I intended to move by without intruding on his thoughts, but he heard my footfalls on the muddy, rutted road and came toward me.

"Thought I'd say goodbye to Jake alone," he said. "Relatives had a private funeral arrangement anyway. I guess you didn't know Jake."

"No, I heard you and some others speak of him."

"He was quite a man. For some time, he was a State Trooper, then when his father died, he came back to the farm and ran a sawmill as well. "

"How did he run a farm and a sawmill?"

"Well, without a herd of milkers he wasn't so strapped for time; just a feed farm raising primarily corn, oats, and alfalfa. The farm wasn't the big anyhow, probably made more on the sawmill, or should have."

"Why 'should have'?"

"Well, he played a different game. I think he almost gave the lumber away. In fact, at times I'm sure he did, just to help someone out. I don't think he left much, monetarily that is ... I remember him sayin' about the only thing he brought home from life's labors was the mud on his feet."

"Any immediate family?"

"No. Wife died a few years ago. There were no children. Jack and I used to fish quite a bit on Sunday afternoons. We spent hours of nothing waiting for a fish we could lie about. Actually, we enjoyed the peace and tranquility of lake and countryside. It didn't matter much whether the fish obliged or not, and when you conversed with Jake there was always a lift of spirit. Maybe it was a mistake goin' up to the cemetery this mornin'. Might have been better to pull the curtain and figure we said goodbye the last day we were together on the lake."

For a moment he stopped, looked back at the cemetery, and fell silent. I moved on a few steps and waited. As he turned toward me again I saw a smile cross his face as he said, "One day Jake was bailin' alfalfa near the main road and I had stopped for a few minutes to pass the time 'a day when a car pulled up and a guy jumped out and asked directions to Rose Hill. 'Well,' Jake replied, 'ya go down this road until - no that won't do, better if ya went back to the first right - no, that won't do either.' Jake scratched his head. 'Ya know, I don't think ya can get there from here."

Henty laughed and I joined in.

"One time," Henty said, "Jake was in the fields when a sudden storm swept over the hill and started to drench the area. Jake remembered he had left his bedroom window open. By the time he got back, his bed was soaked. He said, 'I always did want one of them waterbeds but I don't think they make them that way.'"

"Too bad we never met. He had a good sense of humor," I said.

"Yeah, and then some. He was also a philosopher of sorts. One time he told me many of the living are really dead. I questioned his statement and he said, 'Well, look at it this way, a lot of people just sit around doin' nothin'. They aren't really livin', just existin'.' Some people do more livin' in one year than others do in twenty."

"He had a point there," I said.

Henty continued, "Shortly after his wife died, I remember him sayin', 'Ya know, it's hard enough to plan how you're gonna live, but harder to plan how you're gonna die.' Yeah, he could be serious, but it was his sense of humor that carried the day. Actually, I think he picked himself up with it as well as friends. Come to think of it, one day when we were out in the boat, he said something to that effect. I believe he said, 'If I couldn't laugh at myself I'd 'a died long ago.' He will be missed by a lot of people." Henty looked at me, smiled, and said, "Why is it good men like him pass on, while bums like you and I remain?"

THE FIVE-DOLLAR DOG

I was six years old when "Ginger" came into my life. His coat was brown - various shades, with a touch of black on his shoulders. A neighbor's Airedale had a litter of pups, and after pleading with my father, he gave the man five dollars and Ginger became part of our family. Ginger is a female name and yet our dog was a male. We thought the name appropriate because he was so full of life, constantly alert. The name was all right with Ginger for he answered faithfully to the calling the rest of his life.

Ginger's father, we were told, was a straight-haired Airedale. However, Ginger had long curly hair that for the most part lay flat on his body. I remember measuring some strands on his head that were over five inches in length. I'm certain this heavy coat had great bearing on his behavior in winter's snows.

As I grew older and my horizons widened, so in turn did Ginger's, for he was usually at my side. When I began skating at Onondaga Park, he joined in the action too, often following me around an expansive area north of the bath house. Sometimes he would lie on a nearby snow bank and watch intently until his restless energy had to be expended. Then he would race across the ice to pay me a visit. His headlong dash frequently ended in a slide, tripping up unwary skaters. Perhaps he considered it part of the game. No doubt he saw many a skater fall, so why worry about a few more? Rearing up on his hind legs, placing his forepaws on my chest, with his tongue lolling from his mouth, he would laugh in my face. I found it difficult to punish him.

In a fold in the hills, a long mile from our house, lay a pond. As our skating became more proficient, we decided to stir up the blood a bit more. We added sticks and a puck, thus becoming, so we thought, hockey players. Ginger, I found, also had a taste for hockey. From his observation post on a snow bank, he viewed the battle. However, if an errant puck came his way, he seized the opportunity to pounce on it. Puck clenched firmly in his jaws, he pranced around the edge of the pond, knowing pursuit was fruitless. In short order the prize was deposited on the ice and he returned to his post to delight in our frustration. He seemed to know that we were more intent on acquiring the puck to finish our game, and retribution would not be forthcoming.

Some ventures on the ice were not so tame. One early winter, after a few days of sub-freezing temperatures, I decided to see if it was time to start hockey season. The pond was frozen. On the shallow end I could see the bottom through the thin veneer, but it supported my weight. Ginger followed while I shuffled toward the deep end.

At the deep end was an inlet. Thirty yards from it, the ice gave way and I plunged into the freezing water. As I struggled to belly onto the ice, I noticed Ginger edging toward me. I grasped his collar. At that instant a strange thought struck me. Many times the collar had slipped off while trying to get him to the washtub for a bath. Ginger seemed to sense the problem, for he tipped his head back and cradled the collar. Paws slipped a few times, then set. Ginger backed slowly away from the hole and I bellied up onto the ice. Worried the ice might break again under our combined weight, I released my hold on Ginger's collar and bade him go for shore. He started toward it but soon stopped and looked back to see if I was coming. I was moving on all fours. Ginger, assured all was well, continued on, occasionally taking a peek over his shoulder. I reached solid ground still in a crawling position. Possibly Ginger thought this funny, or perhaps he was celebrating my rescue, for he wagged his stubby tail and jumped on me. Since he had pulled me out I didn't mind his antics. Once on my feet I broke into a trot and, with Ginger romping at my side, soon arrived home.

Ginger's love was forthright, no strings attached. His laughing eyes were constant until near the end, when he became lame and no longer able to join me in my travels, then the light faded from his brown eyes. He would look into my face sorrowfully, as if to say, "Be careful, I can't watch over you anymore."

Edwin Lukens

THERE'S GOT TO BE A WAY

(Editor's note – Also published under the title, "Thoughts of imaginary home runs leave this youth minus one tooth." Both editions have been combined.)

Not long ago, I saw a commercial on TV about a little girl who awoke one morning to find the tooth fairy had left a nickel and a package of gum under her pillow. So informed, when I was young, I might have ripped out all my teeth.

Actually, the commercial brought a smile as I recalled a childhood incident. It happened in the early 1930's when we were in the throes of the Depression. Late one Friday afternoon, my older brother and I walked to a small neighborhood grocery store some four blocks away to carry home our weekly order. The grocery list had been dropped off by me earlier in the week on the way to school.

As I followed my brother through the front door of Mr. Mathews' store, my eye came to rest on a small barrel loaded with brown baseball bats. They were just right for a kid my size. I stood transfixed while my brother sidled up to the counter. The only thing I could see in the store were baseball bats.

In a wire rack to one side were three-bar packs of Palmolive soap and a sign: "Buy three bars for twenty-five cents and get a free baseball bat." At the time, soap didn't interest me but I knew mother would be glad to have it. I said to myself, "There's got to be a way to get one of those bats."

Although I carried a peck of potatoes on the trip home, I could take imaginary swings at baseballs and, in my mind's eye, watch them soar far over the left field fence. I arrived home without a solution to my problem.

I awoke the following morning, greeted by a warm sun streaming through the bedroom window. It was a beautiful May day, and being Saturday I knew the boys in the neighborhood would be gathering at the ballpark. I hurried to the breakfast table and started to wolf down the corn flakes. Mother, viewing my smiling countenance, was certain I had forgotten what was on the agenda. "Remember,

Eddie," she said, "you've got a dental appointment at nine this morning."

"Holy cow, Ma, can't we change it to another day?"

"No, your father says that molar has a large cavity along the gum line and needs to be pulled. You know it's been giving you a lot of trouble."

She handed me a dollar. "This will cover it," she said. "Put it in your back pocket and button it."

"But Ma…"

"No buts…Take care of the money. We can buy four pounds of hamburg with that dollar."

In silence I finished breakfast, deep in despair. I remained at the table while mother cleaned up the dishes and then joined father in the backyard to view the fast-blooming flowers.

Finally, I dragged myself into the living room and slouched down in an old easy chair by the front door. The beautiful day, blossoming with great expectations, had suddenly turned sour. I peeked at the mantelpiece clock. Almost time to leave for the dentist. A half-mile walk lay ahead.

My thoughts wandered to the baseball bats in Mr. Mathews' store. Then it struck me. From some little-used nook in my feeble brain came the answer. I quickly headed for the cellar door, bounced down the stairs to my father's workbench, and selected the tool that would unlock my dream. Placing both hands on the pliers, I clamped down on my nemesis. I feared my head might fly off before the tooth was extracted. Eventually it loosened, and I soon ripped it free. Dropping pliers and tooth on the bench, I ran upstairs.

Out the front door and down the street I raced with reckless abandon. With more than a little elation, I noticed several bats were still in the barrel as I entered Mr. Mathews' store. Grabbing a packet of soap and a bat, I strode to the counter and handed the dollar to Mr. Mathews. He smiled as he gave me the change.

I broke the paper strap off the soap and stuffed the cakes in my pockets.

Heading home, I hardly felt the pain in my jaw. Mother would be so happy when I arrived with tooth gone and seventy-five cents besides. I dragged the back of my hand across the corner of my mouth where something seemed to be leaking out. I gave it little thought.

Bounding up the steps and through the front door, I confronted mother in the living room.

"Look what I…"

"Merciful heavens," she said, "what did that dentist do to you? There's blood caked on your mouth and chin." She stepped closer. "Open your mouth," she commanded.

I obliged, opening as wide as I could, proud of the fact that I had extracted the tooth. She peered in, pushed me aside, took one faltering step and collapsed on the davenport. Mother never did care much for the sight of blood. I ran to the back screen door and hollered to my father who was still working in the yard. As he came up the back steps I said, "I think mother fainted. She's in the living room."

He hurried in to find mother sitting up, looking dazed.

"What happened?" he asked.

She lifted a limp arm in my direction and whispered, "Look at him."

For the first time since my return, father scrutinized me closely. He asked, "Didn't the dentist stop the bleeding before he let you go? You've got blood on your face."

I began to feel like George Washington in the cherry tree episode, but I still figured I had a right to be proud of my actions. Smiling broadly I said, "I took it out myself, Pop. Did it down cellar with a pair of pliers. Look what I bought at the store." I emptied my pockets of soap, then held up the bat for father to see, and said, "I got seventy-five cents change, too."

Mother murmured, "Deliver me from evil," and, glancing at father, added, "Take him to the bathroom, look in his mouth, and please wash his face."

We trooped to the bathroom. Father examined my mouth and said, "Quite a mess in there. Don't seem to have a dry hole, though. I believe it's clotted now." He shook a bent right forefinger in my face, a finger broken while catching a baseball game in his youth. As he did so, he said sternly, "Be sure you go to the dentist next time, okay?" A wisp of a smile crossed his face as he finished saying it.

"Okay," I answered.

All seemed right with the world, at least as far as father and I were concerned, but for several days mother looked at me rather strangely and kept her distance as if I had the plague.

THROUGH THE MISTS OF TIME

As I played a record on an old Magnavox an aunt had given me, my thoughts shed the years to a time long ago when I was young. I seem to recollect my father telling me of an episode concerning a good friend named Lyon. I do not recall his first name.

On the record was a march entitled, "The Regime of Sambre and Meuse." It was composed by a Frenchman in honor of an American Marine regiment that stopped the German army at the gates of Paris during World War I. I seem to recollect Lyon was in that regiment and his outfit held it until the French could support them, and deny the German army from entering Paris.

If my memory serves me correctly, I think the taxicabs of Paris were put into use to rush men to the front. I believe that band of nondescripts became known as "The Taxicab Army."

At this point in my story, I decided to check the garage loft, as it came to mind that I had seen something there that once belonged to Lyon. As I ransacked the loft, I came upon a barracks bag that was given to my father to store and protect a tent. Although faded to some degree, on the side I could still make out the [text is halfway cut off here at bottom of page] name M.L. Lyons and on the flap, U.S.M.C.

Even though a multitude of years have gone by, the story my father related to me in my youth did hold true. It was not a figment of my imagination.

The march, "The Regiment of Sambre and Meuse," is one of the finest marches I have ever heard. It is a well-deserved tribute to the splendid Marine regiment that so gallantly held the line at the gates of Paris.

In heaven where Lyon now resides, I give a nod and my heartfelt thanks for a job well done and for his friendship to my father.

THE LAST TROUT

He was propped against the trunk of a large, weather-beaten cedar tree. His fly rod, braced on one knee, slanted out over the sparkling water of a quiet pool. Dickie was 12 years old, sunken-cheeked, hollow-eyed, and frail of frame. A serious illness had taken its toll. He had coaxed for some time to go fishing. Finally, with some misgivings, his father consented. He was bundled up to protect against a cool, spring day, although sun shone on occasion, through patches of blue between billowy white clouds.

As he watched a faint smile cross Dickie's pale face, it eased his anxiety somewhat. A promise of an hour's fishing at his favorite pool had been his son's reward. He wondered at the final result. It would be a shame if the boy's efforts availed him nothing. He prayed some trout, however small, would fall prey to Dickie's bait, although it seemed rather hopeless. The stream was clear and low and he knew that his son's efforts, as well as his own, had been unproductive here since Dickie caught his trophy trout two summers ago. He thought, "He's still dreaming of the big one and thinks history will repeat itself." How many times through the years had he returned to so many favorite spots with their pleasant memories?

The minutes were slipping by, while a deeply concerned father stood nervously on the bank, waiting for the hour to come to a close. Then, to his eternal wonder, a phantom in the crystal pool straightened the slack line, the pole bowed as Dickie set the hook, and the battle was on. The pool was small and the fish stayed within its confines; thus, very little line left the reel. The pulsating fly rod was taking the brunt of the fight, and Dickie, putting pressure expertly on the line, was begrudging the trout every previously gained inch.

The communication between Dickie and the trout through line and pole was like an electric charge. His face, now alive, changed expressions with every rise and fall of the engagement. Dickie's persistence was paying off, the rushes became shorter, until finally a beautiful brook trout lolled on its side close by the grassy bank. Here, his father assisted the operation by reaching down, grasping the slippery trout, and swinging him clear of his sanctuary. He deposited the fish beside the tired but supremely happy boy.

By some standards the brookie was not a giant, yet it measured over 14 inches. Most importantly, it gave Dickie great enjoyment.

As the late afternoon shadows lengthened, Dickie, with trout on a forked stick, was cradled in his father's arms and carried triumphantly from the quiet pool. Through cedar and willow, across a meadow, to the waiting car they went, father and son as one.

The following afternoon at approximately the same time he caught his fish, Dickie passed away. He died while sleeping, a wisp of a smile on his lips; perhaps he was dreaming of his trout. In his heaven, let there be a quiet pool where brookies abound.

THE TERRIBLE TOLL

A short time ago, I spent a few days in Gloucester, Mass. At harbor's edge stands the Fishermen's Memorial. It is a statue of a helmsman keeping his craft on course. The statue is a memorial to all fishermen who ventured forth from Gloucester since settling in 1623 and lost their lives.

The inscription reads: "They that go down to the sea in ships." It is taken from Psalm 107, verse 23, line 24, which reads as follows:

> "They that go down to the sea in ships,
> That do business in great waters;
> These see the works of the Lord,
> And his wonders in the deep."

To see the bronze plaques surrounding the statue, with the names of fishermen who fought angry seas and never returned to port was appalling. Four thousand souls; now and forever the sea will hold them.

Below one plaque, someone had placed a bouquet and a card listing two names. I found the names on the plaque and noticed they had perished recently.

Some two hundred yards from the Fishermen's Memorial stands another monument. It is a bronze statue of a woman on a rock, a young daughter held in one arm, while the other rests on her son standing beside her.

The memorial reaches beyond Gloucester to the wives of fishermen and mariners the world over for their unselfish contribution to family and community. It is a tribute and reminder that while men go out to see, women wait - with strength - keeping families together and staying active in the community. They stood on the rock, hoping and praying their men would return from each ocean voyage. There was always the possibility of extended grievous loss to family and friends.

Lord comfort all who have lost loved ones to the sea.

THE MISSED POT OF GOLD

In the thirties during the throes of the Great Depression, when money was more than scarce, our family was able to enjoy a two-week vacation on Skaneateles Lake. This high point in our lives was made possible when my father's oldest brother sent money to cover expenses.

Alf Randall, a farmer on Pine Grove Road, had recently built two cottages. We rented one for $9 a week. Alf had a daughter with three children living at the farm, and we became good friends with all, as we frequently came up to the farmhouse for vegetables and eggs. We returned the next year and I remember father brought some little gifts for the children.

Some years went by, and then the terrible years of World War II descended upon us. My brother became a captain and company commander. He hopped from island to island in the Pacific. I traveled through Africa and Italy.

While we were in service, Alf Randall got in touch with my father and told him he was selling the cottage we had rented. The price was $1,000 and Alf wanted my father to have first crack at it. He told Alf he would get in touch with my brother and me, then let him know. It took considerable time to communicate with us and although he said we would be able to handle the transaction, the offer was turned down.

Father had reservations. He worried that something might happen to us and everything would come to an end. His worries were nearly justified, as my brother was severely wounded in the battle for Okinawa during the last days of the war. He was in a coma for two weeks and woke up in a base hospital on Guam, where he had started out during the war. He was permanently disabled. I made it through without too much trouble.

Soon after my father passed on the offer, Alf called and said he sold the cottage for $1,100 dollars. The extra $100 was a considerable amount at the time. I think Alf was being nice to us, as we cleaned the cottage before leaving, bought produce and, as I said before, became good friends with my family.

A chance was missed; perhaps it could have been called the chance of a lifetime. Then again, there were many pleasant memories.

ONE FUNNY INDIAN

Edwin Lukens

While working as a fishing guide for Laurentian Air Services in northern Canada, I came in contact with Philip. He was a Montagnais Indian from southern Labrador, knowledgeable on wilderness ways, and bowman in my freighter canoe. The freighter canoes were 20 feet long, had a 5-foot beam, a square tail, and were powered by Johnson 10-horse motors. We had paddles but they were almost useless in the river where we fished. Some of the rapids were nearly a quarter mile wide with roaring white water. Paddles would only be good to keep the canoe in line if the motor quit. However, not being able to move faster than the current, left you at the mercy of the river and impending disaster on the rocks. The bowman was mainly utilized for checking rocks, landings, and assisting fishing parties.

One day, we started down a rapid and some 100 yards ahead was a ridge of rock barely under the surface. The force of water against it threw a haymow nearly two stories high. Philip turned to me with a big smile on his face and hollered, "We go!" I hollered back, "No we don't go!" I quickly turned the canoe toward the near riverbank and the quiet water of a small back eddy.

Philip was a jovial Indian who understood the wilderness. He was a hunter and fisherman who took care of family needs. Why he looked forward to battling that wall of white water that would probably have tossed the canoe end-over-end, I do not know. He could not swim, and Indians and Eskimos do not readily take to swimming. Water temperature in that area hovers around the 30-degree mark in early summer and stays in the 40s through July and August. Once, during the first few days of July, I was on the shore of Michikamau Lake in Labrador, ice was piled up on islands and in a few bays.

I cannot help but smile when I remember another escapade with Phil. We were taking care of a fishing party consisting of two surgeons, a biologist, and his son. We were located on a massive promontory of rock that stuck out some 50 yards into the river. While watching primarily brook trout and landlocked salmon, a large lake trout around 20 pounds was landed. The rock point had many fissures on it, and the fellow who caught the laker set his expensive graphite fly rod across one of these fissures. Before he could remove the lure, the fish flopped and came down on the precise spot where the rod bridged the gap, snapping it in two. That didn't set well with the fisherman. Philip, however, was enjoying it immensely. He did a little jig, looked and pointed a waving arm skyward, and laughed. Evidently he figured the god and protector of namaycush (lake trout) had served retribution for catching the fish.

That night at the dinner table, Philip was sitting across from me. I caught his eye, smiled, looked and pointed toward heaven, and said, "Namaycush." Philip started laughing like mad as I joined in, recollecting the incident.

To this day, I am amazed at the episode with Philip in the rapids. I cannot comprehend his willingness to challenge that maelstrom, where no glimmer of hope to escape its wrath existed.

I trust he is still roaming the wilderness and laughing at the antics of man and beast.

HANDS ACROSS THE HEMISPHERES

In Australia many years ago, I had one of my most moving experiences. At the time I was with the American Masters track and field team that had come to compete in the World Games. Open days before the competition gave me a chance to move around a bit; however, my stirring experience came at Melbourne University, where I was residing in a dormitory.

I met Lyle Harvey, who was in charge of maintenance at the university. As we talked, he mentioned World War II, possibly because he thought some of the American men had served in that conflagration. I told him that I had traveled through Africa with the British forces. We talked about it for a while, and then he excused himself and disappeared into another room, but soon returned with two paperback books. He said one was a story of two young men who had traveled across the wild north coast and the other dealt with the Aussie campaign in Africa.

Although I hadn't known him long, he handed me the books. I was quite surprised and thanked him for his generosity. Then he related to me how his father had been severely wounded in one of the last battles the Aussies fought. As he spoke, I could see he was deeply affected by the incident. He said that when it happened, a United States Army outfit was close by and their medics actually came to his aid. The story became more amazing as he continued. The Americans must have thought his injuries were so severe that certain treatment was needed quickly, and where that could be attained. His father was placed on a plane with some United States casualties and flown to a hospital in the New York City area. There, surgeons were able to save him. Probably no one back home knew what transpired because long lapses in communication prevailed in wartime.

While still under therapy but able to walk, he was taken under wing by Americans who were also recovering from injuries. They paid his way wherever they went.

I was transfixed by the story, but what happened next moved me deeply. Lyle held out his hand to give me something and I reacted. Into my palm was placed a gold-winged insignia pin. He said, "It was my father's and I want you to have it."

Stunned by his action, some time passed before I regained my composure. I said something to the effect that I had nothing to do with your father's recovery and his pin belongs in your hands. He said, "No, you must take it. This is something I want to do. In some small way I am thanking Americans for their great concern and care given my father."

I was amazed at the Australian's gratitude and gift to me. The pin with the inscription, Australian Military Forces, rests on a desk in my den. It was a noble gesture and will live with me forever.

To the Americans who knew the dire circumstances of the Aussie's injury and never wavered a moment in giving aid - to all those along the way that so nobly advanced those great lines: "I am my brother's keeper." I give belated heartfelt thanks.

THOUGHTS ON A VETERANS DAY

The creeping paralysis of time obliterates past reference points, and yet I find not only cities but small towns in North Africa still escape the veil of years; places like Oran, Arzew, El Bir, Algiers, Bougie, Orleansville, Constantine, and Philippeville.

We landed at Oran and soon progressed eastward. Sometime later I remember reading an account of Oran Landing, how it was met with slight resistance and in two days fell to United States forces. It may have been a light engagement, but just outside the city our convoy passed an American cemetery and I noticed several hundred white crosses that made me think otherwise.

The mind sorts and stores many things, some of a trivial nature. One such incident comes to mind. Somewhere along the road to Algiers one rainy night, the convoy came down out of the Atlas Mountains and stopped in an irrigated valley. I could see the outline of what I believed to be the fruit trees in the murk. I told the men I was going to check the trees for oranges as I jumped out of the truck, and to holler like mad when the convoy started up again.

Reaching into the wet branches, fruit was found and stuffed into the raincoat and all other pockets. I headed back, scrambled into the truck and passed by booty around. Somebody snapped a flashlight on and deflated my ego. There were oranges all right, but green as grass and bitter. My so-called friends threatened to throw me off the tuck, evidently figuring I failed on my mission to bring back something edible.

Eventually, we arrived in Algiers and set tents on a hillside overlooking the harbor. The war had passed by and, except for a few air raids on the harbor works, all was quiet. Two weeks went by and then it was off down the road toward Tunisia.

Another incident etched in my memory happened as we neared Constantine. We were high in the mountains on a tortuous road that cut back on itself time and again. The sun had been shining throughout the day, but late in the afternoon clouds began sifting through the peaks and a persistent drizzling rain soon followed. We stopped, pulled tarps over stays, and tied them down. At least we would have some protection against the elements. In short order the surface of the narrow dusty road turned to greasy mud.

Our truck started to fishtail on the crowned road as we rounded a sharp right turn. I watched the truck immediately behind skate toward the left side. There were no protective devices, not even shoulders, and the terrain fell away abruptly. The truck dropped off, turned over, spewing men out of the back as it crashed down the mountainside. It rolled for 200 yards before it came to a halt with a shattering moan of a man who had been thrown out close to the road. Before the truck ended its deadly journey, men were scrambling over the rocks to find and care for survivors.

I thought of the dark hand the rain had played - not only the slick road, but also the sheltering tarp we placed over the men a short time before now acted as a trap. Fate, an eternal hunter, dealt them a cruel blow.

Not one man jumped from the truck before it rolled. Evidently, they were not alerted to the greater danger of the sliding truck. Then, too, the men were accustomed to skidding vehicles on muddy roads. When it rolled it was too late to escape.

A soldier could die a better death than have life beaten and crushed out of him. There are many subtle ways of dying in a war. For most of the men in the truck the war had come to an end . . . and so did life.

It happened almost 70 years ago in the mountains of North Africa near Constantine. And I cannot forget.

THE TRIP OF A LIFETIME

Words of Wisdom

Recently, I headed west to view some of our national treasures. While traveling nearly 9,000 miles, I was rewarded time and time again by scenic wonders.

Yosemite, set aside in 1890, is one of the most beautiful parks. Within its 750,000 acres are three stands of giant Sequoia trees, a falls with a 2,425-foot drop, and 800 miles of trails. It ranges from 2,000 feet above sea level to 13,000 feet.

Yellowstone National Park, another treasure, includes many hot springs (Old Faithful being one), and an abundance of rivers, lakes, and mountains. There is also the Grand Canyon of the Yellowstone to enthrall all who venture there.

Close to the south end of Yellowstone lies Grand Teton National Park, with a mountain range most photographed of all. The snow-capped peaks rise to 14,000 feet. Along the valley floor, the Snake River winds its way. It is indeed an awe-inspiring sight.

The Grand Canyon, Zion, and Bryce have their cathedral spires and changing color patterns in sun and shadow. I heard the Grand Canyon came into being when a Scot lost a nickel and in search of it, did a little digging. I don't quite believe that; the canyon is so vast I'm sure it would have taken at least two Scots to create it. It is quite a trough, a mile deep, and from the rim I watched a thunderstorm roll toward me. It was strange to look down at the flashing lightning.

In California and Oregon, I gazed at the tallest trees in the world. There is a differentiation concerning these wondrous giants that grow primarily on the western slope of the Sierra Nevada Mountains. In this area are found Sequoias and Redwoods. They are truly incredible trees for the eye to behold. The Redwood is the tallest tree, with one recorded around 360 feet, which is taller than the Statue of Liberty. Coming from a seed as tiny as a tomato seed, the trees in maturity may weigh 500 tons and have a lifespan of 2,000 years. The bark is about 12 inches thick; root may penetrate to a 13-foot depth and spread to 80 feet, with a trunk 40 feet in circumference. Sequoias have been found to be a height of 311 feet, bark about 31 inches thick and a base about the same as the Redwood. I did, however, come upon one that a ranger told me was 54 feet around. Sequoias have been known to live up to 3,200 years.

We are fortunate to have so many areas where the beautiful and rare are commonplace. It is surprising to realize that the Interior Department manages about one of every five acres across the country. Included in this territory are 387 national park units and 544 wildlife refuges. Almost half of some states are national forest land or wildlife reserve areas. Montana, Idaho, and Oregon are in this category. In New York, we are blessed to have the Adirondack State Park, which is the largest state park in the nation. In landmass, it has six million acres - making it bigger than the Grand Canyon, Glacier, and Yellowstone Parks combined.

To Teddy Roosevelt we owe a debt of gratitude. The prospect of big game hunting had initially brought him west. This might seem contrary to the principles of conservation, but he had the vision and understanding to protect the treasure we have - the scenic beauty of the land and forests.

As time went on he became more and more alarmed at the damage done to land and wildlife. Originally, he established two open range ranches, and in 1901 the US Forest Service. By signing the Antiquities Act in 1906, he proclaimed 18 national monuments. He also obtained Congressional approval for the establishment of five national parks and 51 wildlife refuges and set aside land for national forests. He is remembered with a national park that bears his name and honors his memory of that great conservationist. I visited the park in North Dakota.

In our wonderful parks and preserves you can also glory in animal life. It is relatively easy to see elk, buffalo, moose, antelope, and both whitetail and mule deer. With some luck, a coyote, wolf, black bear, or grizzly may come to view. Bird life is quite abundant as well.

It is important for us to guard against infringement on our scenic wonderlands. There is also a need for funds to clean up debris, fix roads and buildings, and take care of other problems that involve our US Forest Service.

Along the way, many sites of significance beckon, historical and otherwise. At Monterey Bay on the California coast you might visit the fine aquarium and check out Fisherman's Wharf. Along the Oregon coast south of Florence, ride a dune buggy and enjoy the sea, forest, and dunes. Believe it or not, there are dunes that reach 385 feet in height. North of Florence lies the largest sea cave in the world. In soars to the height of a 12-story building and is long as a football field. Stellar sea lions, weighing up to a ton, call it home. On the rock ledges outside the cave, you might see about a hundred more.

If you have the chance the visit our scenic treasures, do not hesitate. You will be rewarded many times over.

I might add that a substantial savings can be attained when you reach the age of 62. For a one-time fee of $10, you receive a Golden Age Passport, which alleviates payment forever in your travels through our national parks.

GUIDING THE GOOD DOCTOR

One day in late summer, while working as a guide for Laurentian Air Services in Canada, I met a surgeon from Philadelphia by the name of Stayman. He had come into camp to fish, but also to check the Grenfell Mission in Nain, an Eskimo village on the Labrador coast.

Dr. Wilfred Grenfell, who was both physician and missionary, established the mission. In 1889, with the aid of another doctor, he fitted out the first hospital ship for the North Sea Fisheries, arranging for mission vessels on the sea and establishing homes for fishermen on land from the Bay of Biscay to Iceland. In 1892, he went to Labrador, where he worked as a missionary and physician for 42 years in the service of 10,000 or more white inhabitants and 5,000 Eskimos and Indians.

At the Grenfell Mission in Nain, an English nurse was in attendance. Some 600 to 700 Eskimos were located there. The

Canadian government likes to have a base of operations for them so that they can attend to their welfare. There was a little store in town. However, supplies were brought in from the sea as there were no roads.

We made two trips to the mission and on the first one, I couldn't help noticing a big, beautiful husky dog that accompanied the nurse. I thought he might bite my hand off, but he seemed to like an ear rub.

On the second floatplane trip to Nain, Dr. Stayman took care of an Eskimo that managed to shoot himself in the foot. Some early seals had some into the bay and, in the ensuing hunt, the damage was done. Seals were hunted from the late summer through winter and then the Inuits netted Arctic char in river mouths along the coast. The fish were cleaned, flattened, salted, and packed in barrels, the weight being some 240 pounds. Eskimos would put their mark on the barrels and a trawler picked them up and eventually payment was received.

One early morning, Dr. Stayman and I were fishing on the coast a half mile inland from Tusiak Fiord, a relatively small river made a short run from lake to sea. At the head end, lake water dropped over a seven-foot falls into a wild stretch of river but for a holding pool below falls. Char by the thousands would run the river, rest in the holding poo, then jump the falls and spawn in the many streams that ran down to the lake. The holding pool was about 75 yards long, 60 yards wide, and some 10 feet deep and alive with fish.

On a rocky point below the falls, we worked the pool for about two hours, bringing char in and releasing them. Arms were weary and we sat down laughing at our pleasant predicament.

My days with Dr. Stayman were short in number and although long ago, they are well remembered. I hope he still bends a rod over a fishing hole. Good luck, Doc.

DESTINATION: EDUCATION

The new school bus terminal moved into last December is greatly appreciated by all. Space denied in the old building is no longer a problem, and putting up with lack of heat in winter's cold is a thing of the past.

Terry Smith is in her 40th year as dispatcher, but she is certainly knowledgeable concerning the responsibilities of drivers. She knows the system from the ground up, having been a driver for 14 years.

Terry told me of the intricacies that exist in keeping to a schedule, and that means fighting the wicked winter weather. In the extreme cold, the buses started because they were plugged in, as Terry called it, meaning the engines were warmed. An assistant dispatcher, Peter Williams, also handles bus breakdowns and checks progress with mechanics.

Some of the routes covered by the Skaneateles School System are quite extensive. It reaches down the west side of Skaneateles Lake beyond Mandana and on the east side to the Spafford fire barn. It meshes with the Auburn, Homer, Marcellus, and Jordan-Elbridge systems. There are other duties involved besides regular runs. There is extensive utilization of buses for field trips and athletic events.

The everyday school schedule requires shifts. Drivers arrive between 6:15 and 6:30 AM and carry through to 9:15 AM. Another makes four runs from 11:15 AM to 12:45 PM caring for kindergarten children. In the afternoon, students are homeward bound from 2 to 4:45 PM. An activities bus leaves the school at 3 PM.

There are 20 drivers, about three-quarters of them women, ready for duty, and one emergency or standby driver available at the terminal. In total, there are 24 buses with three having lifts for the handicapped children and two mechanics to keep the fleet in order.

I spoke with Peter Payntar, who not too long ago became a driver. He mentioned a written test concerning rules of the road, and also drives around Auburn to familiarize himself with city problems, including stops at railroad crossings. He told me that when a driver was hired, he would accompany the retiree on his route for a while so problems did not occur.

Their facility and all it encompasses is there for the express purpose of taking care of students. Safety in transport is by far the most important. It is imperative that pupils do not distract drivers in their duties. It is problem enough handling buses especially on snow-covered roads.

Parents' most precious possessions rest in the hands of the operators of the buses, and those operators are cognizant of the fact that they are part of the chain to make sure dreams are realized.

THE LONG ROAD HOME

The day was hot and humid for late April, and as I skirted Pogey Pond, the pull of the clear cool water was like a magnet to me. My dog, Ginger, a large black and brown, curly-haired Airedale, was close on my heels as I turned from the well-worn path and slanted down a patch of scrub willow that bordered the pond. Stopping in a secluded spot, I started to peel off my sweat-stained clothes. Ginger gave me a knowing look that started his stub tail wagging. Ginger loved the water as few dogs do, and while I thrashed around, he followed close in my wake, coughing from time to time as he swallowed his usual mouthful or two of water.

Refreshed, I returned to my clothes and, in short order, was ready to head homeward. It was then that I heard Ginger whimper. Looking back, I watched him try desperately to claw his way up the steep bank from water's edge to my side. Painfully, he approached on stiff legs; then, only a few steps away, collapsed completely. No doubt his advancing years and the cold water had taken their toll.

I gathered him up in my arms and staggered up the incline to the path above. Here I set him down, thinking that on level ground he might travel under his own power, but to no avail. So once again I picked him up and started down the path. Ginger weighed more than 70 pounds and over two miles of primarily rough terrain lay before me. However, I tackled the task willingly, for Ginger had given me 11 years of faithful companionship. If I was going home, he was going too.

I swung off the path, across a field north of the pond, gaining 50 yards or so each carry. A road was crossed, then I followed the stream that was the outlet of the pond. Now I carried him back through areas where he had frolicked a hundred times or more in all seasons. As I set him down on a grassy bank next to the stream, he looked wistfully at the quiet pool below. He glanced at me and I could almost hear him say, "I remember this place. You dammed the stream here to make it deep enough to swim."

It was also the spot where first I saw Ginger hunt crayfish. In the shallows at the head of the pool, a crayfish was disturbed. When it darted to sanctuary under a rock, Ginger decided he wanted to take another look at this strange creature, so he turned the rock over with his paw and the hunt continued. If a crayfish scooted under a rock too large to move, Ginger soon found that if he moved enough rocks, eventually another crayfish would be uncovered. Often as they darted away, Ginger lunged, creating a shower of spray as he tried to grab it in his mouth. All he got for his trouble was a mouthful of water.

Resting on the bank, I had the feeling Ginger realized he might never see this place again. Perhaps with the weight of years he understood his life had nearly run its course. The thought disturbed me. I cradled Ginger in my arms and turned my back on the pool.

A patch of scrub apple interlaced with grassy lanes where cattle grazed was traversed. Carries became shorter, rest periods longer. Now before me lay a woods and the most formidable terrain. My pace slowed as I feared pitching forward and hurting my companion.

Ginger seemed to realize he was a heavy burden and tried several times to walk but legs would not do his bidding. He looked at me sadly, head bowed, eyes rolled up, as if apologizing for the trouble he was causing me. However, each time I started to pick him up his stub tail wagged as if thanking me for not leaving him behind.

The woods passed. I came to a road and, much relieved, shuffled along the hard level surface. Eventually a small park on the edge of town was reached. Here at a drinking fountain I refreshed myself and, placing my thumb over the top of the fountain, squirted water to Ginger nearby as he gratefully caught it on the fly. For some time I rested from the long haul before attacking the half mile that lay ahead.

Journey continued, I gained the top of a steep hill. Only a quarter mile to go now. Level ground, but for the last leg, a short downhill grade to the house.

Finally, after two and a half hours of travel, I struggled up the front porch steps and lightly deposited my furry load. Weary from the long journey, I sat down on the top step, then laid back just in time to catch a wet tongue in the face.

BEWARE OF TROUT STREAMS

Bill Jennings and Dorie Atkins are about to get hitched. That's the big news around here; big news not as a surprise, but rather because it had been a long time coming . . . several years to be exact.

Bill was tall, broad-shouldered, and had a wealth of blond hair that crowned a square-jawed handsome face. Dorie was a slender brunette of average height. Most people figured they came out about even as far as looks were concerned. Come Saturday they would tie the knot, and on this beautiful late spring evening, a rehearsal was scheduled for seven o'clock in the town church.

Bill shuffled across the yard, squeezed into his old battered Chevy sedan, and headed slowly down the back road. He approached the bridge over his favorite trout stream. Bringing the vehicle to a halt on the wooden structure, he surveyed the deep dark hole on the downstream side. As he pondered the wedding and his possible loss of fishing time, a feeding trout dimpled the surface. Simultaneously, two more came to the roof of their home and found supper. Bill looked at his watch. He had more than enough time to travel the few miles to town.

He moved the car to the shoulder of the road. Quickly, he alighted, opened the trunk and grabbed his fly rod and canvas creel that was there throughout the season. Line, leader, and even a Blue Dun dry fly were connected. Piecing the pole together was all that was necessary. The boots were back at the house and the clothes did not fit the purpose, but he would only fish the hole and stay high and dry on the bank.

Three trout came to the creel. Several more casts produced nothing. He eyed the placid pool below and did not hesitate. Two more fish were caught as he lost himself in the electric communication of surging trout through pole and line . . . crystal-laughing water over graveled bottom and song of redwings and meadowlarks.

Rounding a bend, he wandered into a section of fast runs and small pools with sparse scrub willow along undercut banks. A large brown trout bowed the rod. Eventually it tired and Bill stepped to water's edge to land the fish. His lead foot crashed through the roof of a muskrat tunnel and he ended up on his knees in two feet of water. The trout was still on and in short order was retrieved. As he cleaned himself and checked his fly rod, around a bush a short distance away came a lone fisherman.

"Hi, Bill. Don't you think it's a little early to go swimmin'?" he said.

"Yeah, Red, it does seem a trifle cold. I had an idea I might take a float trip downstream and perhaps do some trolling."

"I'm surprised to see you on the stream. I thought your girlfriend broke you of fishin'."

"Good night!" Bill exclaimed as he looked at his watch. "It's after 7:30 and I was supposed to be at church for a rehearsal at seven o'clock. Dorie will go nuts. She'll kill me."

Red laughed and said, "There goes another wedding lost to a fish pole. Look at the bright side. Now you can go fishin' all the time."

Bill sat down on the bank, took his shoes off and swished them around in the stream to get the mud out. Hastily he slipped the shoes on again and said, "Red, Lord willin', I may see you again."

"Yeah. Good luck."

Bill ran to his car. He threw the creel with the six trout and pole in the back and took off down the dirt road in a billowing cloud of dust.

The following afternoon, Bill met Red in the town store.

"I see you're still alive," Red said.

"Just barely. Dorie exploded in about three directions . . . bordered on the eruption of a volcano. By this morning, she had calmed down to some degree. However, the wedding's in a state of limbo."

Red was having trouble trying to speak.

Bill said, "What's so doggoned funny? She's worth a few less days on the stream."

Red, now in control of himself, said, "So they were still waiting at the church when you arrived last night?"

"Were they ever - Dorie, her mother and father - like vultures ready to swoop on their prey. It took me about ten minutes to get a word in. I told Dorie not to get so mad, as I wasn't out with another woman, but just fishin' and lost track of time. That didn't go over too well, but when I offered to give her half the fish..."

SHED ONE TEAR

When I read about the earthquake in Italy some time back, more than 200,000 people homeless and thousands dead, I sympathized with their plight, perhaps more because of an affinity to the country. I spent two years there during another time of devastation ... World War II. Many of the cities and towns hardest hit by the earthquake were also hard hit by the war in 1943 and 1944. Places like

Naples, Avellino, Caserta, Santa Maria, Capua, and many more come to mind. Some nestled in the mountains behind Salerno and others along the road to Casino and Rome.

My thoughts rolled back the years and fastened themselves on two singular incidents that involved fate, the eternal hunter.

We had in my outfit a sergeant by the name of Neil Carlson. He was tall, slender, had dark curly hair and a smile with character. It was there in troubled times. Carlson for some reason beyond my recollection was obsessed with the idea of becoming a warrant officer. His goal was not attained in our outfit, but after a transfer to another, his dream was realized.

The first morning in his new status, he decided to stretch his legs. A masked silence hung over the battlefield; an ominous silence that was not forever . . . or could be. Leaving the shelter of a battle-scarred farmhouse, he strolled a timeworn path just below a ridge, basking in sunshine and elation of his promotion. His outfit was dug in along the south bank of the Volturno River, north of Caserta and across the river in the German positions. Probably an enemy soldier in an observation post focused his field glasses on him and figured where there was one soldier, no doubt there were more. He rang in the artillery. The first shot from an 88 landed right beside Carlson, killing him about ten times over, bringing an end to his elation and sunny days.

Once the main road north of Naples slants up the steep hillside from the port area, it runs straight and level for miles. Trees line the sides, but do not arch over it. Just off the road a short distance from Naples lay an airfield. It was a fighter base. The planes flew cover for bombers and also strafed and dive-bombed enemy targets.

On a bright summer day, a pilot came through the gate, bag in hand, and proceeded to thumb a ride toward Naples. His name was Gary Barnes and he had almost twice the number of missions necessary to go home, and so he was off to the states. The first vehicle; an empty ambulance picked Barnes up and in the conversation, he told the driver he was a P47 Thunderbolt pilot. He also said that he would meet some other flyers in Naples and then be driven to another airfield to start the first leg home.

One of our men was driving a weapons carrier to the port for supplies. He was less than a half mile from the ambulance when a lone Messerschmitt came down the line strafing. Bullets ripped into the weapons carrier, but the driver was not injured. Sweeping in behind the ambulance, the pilot of the Messerschmitt did not hesitate to fire, and in the deadly hail of metal, wounded the driver and killed Barnes.

The weapons carrier was fair game, but not the ambulance. The pilot of the Messerschmitt could not have made a mistake. The large red crosses against a white background covered the sides, back, and top of the vehicle. Evidently it made a better target.

What a travesty. Barnes faced death in nearly a hundred missions, only to die in an ambulance on the way home.

BEAR WITH ME

My father and I were staying in a cabin on the shore of Kipawa Lake in Canada. A short distance away, a fellow was building a cottage on a steep bank. The front was supported by piling, and some seven feet off the ground, the frame was up, but no windows or doors were in place. For some reason, he had a trapdoor in the floor.

One day he brought some lumber over and decided to push it through the trap onto the ground floor. However, when he removed the door, he found that he had a guest. Staring him in the face was a black bear of some three hundred pounds. The poor fellow realized it wouldn't do much good to argue who had rights to the cottage, so he beat a hasty retreat. Eventually he returned and peeked through a rear window opening and found his guest had gone. I guess the bear wasn't sold on the cottage.

In the Labrador-New Quebec wilderness where I had taken trips and guided fishing parties for Laurentian Air Services, I became involved in another adventure. Dr. Banfield, curator of the Canadian National Museum at the time, wanted a barren ground grizzly bear for the museum, and an editor of a magazine in New York City wanted the story.

I had traversed this territory many times and had never seen a grizzly. I believe people had seen brown colorations of the black bear and thought they were grizzlies. It would have been quite a story to find them east of the Hudson Bay. Fishing for Atlantic salmon was also enjoyed at the time.

I wasn't delinquent concerning bear watching, however, as those animals frequented the banks of the rivers and lakes. On the exposed areas, blueberries grew on runted bushes and grubs could be found under the rocks along the shore. These foods were welcome additions to the bears' diet. As I fished, a rifle was close at hand, but no grizzly was sighted and the request was therefore not fulfilled.

On another excursion, a pilot and I were checking rivers near the north coast of Canada with a Cessna floatplane, the objective being to find out what kind of fish were indigenous and abundant in any area. If out camps were to be set up, it would also be important to know if the rivers could be navigated to some extent by canoe. After dropping on several rivers, the pilot left me about thirty miles from the north coast and flew back to base. He would pick me up in a few days and, in the meantime, I would make camp and fish the river on foot.

After erecting a small mountain tent and placing everything inside, I grabbed a fishing rod and set off upstream. In short order, a rather serious problem confronted me. Some three hundred yards above camp I sighted a bear with a cub. I doubt the mother bear had ever seen a human being before, and it just eyed me and went about its business. As I did not have a gun, I was intent on giving the bears ample room. As it was late afternoon, I turned back.

Early the following morning, I set out in the same direction again. There was a bend in the river where the two bears had been sighted and a cliff that came down almost to the water's edge.

Intending to check upriver for a few miles and having no desire to come face to face with mother and cub in close quarters, I would carry out accepted procedure - that being singing or whistling as I approached my spot. I decided my singing might well aggravate the bears, so I whistled instead. I passed through without confrontation. Although I did not see them as I rounded the bend, it's also possible that they found my whistling somewhat irritating and headed for more peaceful surroundings.

WHEN SHADOWS FALL

It has been a span of years since I first met Clara and Albert. I was taking a shortcut down a dusty back road when a fresh egg sign caught my eye. Being in low supply, I stopped, ambled up the bank, and headed for the weather-beaten farmhouse that stood some distance away. Nearly to the porch, I was distracted by the movement of a woman off to my right, a small form bending low over a vegetable patch.

"Hello," I said.

The form, lean and wiry, hardened by the endless toil of years, came erect. She turned her head and said, "Howdy."

"Saw the sign, would like to get two dozen eggs."

"Sure thing," she replied, as she wiped her hands on a faded blue apron. It was then I noticed a man seated in a straight-backed wooden chair near the house and lilac bush. As we came closer, I saw that he was shelling peas with great effort. Hands did not do their bidding and head shook slightly from side to side. I was beginning to get the idea that most of the load was carried by the spry elderly woman with snow white hair whom I now followed to the rear of the house. I waited as she opened the screen door and disappeared inside.

At the door again, she leaned; it slapped shut behind her.

"They be 40 cents a dozen for the large ones," she said.

I found the change and paid her. She smiled and I could see the gleam in her eye that seemed to say all was right with the world; I thought to myself - a tough world.

As I turned to go, she added, "If you're ever around these parts again, stop by." I realized she meant for eggs, as no doubt the money was needed.

"I'll try to do that," I said, and headed for the car.

Many times I returned for eggs and also produce that Clara began to sell. We became good friends, and often I lingered to pass the time of day.

Once I arrived on the fifth of July. Noticing the flag was still displayed, I said, "Clara, you can take the flag down now, the Fourth is over."

She looked at it a moment and replied, "You know, it looks just as good on the fifth."

I figured that was a pretty good answer and did not question her further.

Although self-conscious about his disability, Albert eventually entered into the conversation and seemed to enjoy my coming. He never mentioned his problem but one day, as I chatted with Clara, hoe in hand, chopping weeds in her garden, it was answered. She rested for a moment, leaned on the hoe, and gazed wistfully across the fields.

"You know," she said, "we've been here over 50 years. At one time most of the 120 acres we owned was cultivated. Albert worked hard - a fine farm it was - patchwork of crops and a good woodlot, too. That was over 12 years ago. Before his heart attack."

"That's what stopped him?" I asked.

"Well, that, and a few other afflictions. Arthritis in his hands limits him greatly, but he does all he can."

She looked away from the fields, bowed head to her work.

"How much land do you have now, Clara?"

Reckon about two acres. Sold the rest to a farmer down the road. Mainly hays it for cows. The barn's his too, but I kept the shed for my chickens."

"I don't see how you manage, Clara."

"Well, you keep us goin'."

I laughed. "I'm afraid the price of a dozen eggs a week don't pay many bills."

"There are other customers and we freeze vegetables, berries, slices of apples from our two old trees for pies, and put up sauce. We make do."

I kept in touch throughout the next year as Albert's health deteriorated. When the end came, Clara took the shock in stride. But a few weeks later I visited the farm and found for the first time that the spark was gone from her eyes.

Without Albert to walk with, to wait on, to fight for, her life was hollow. Friends came to visit and tried to lift her spirits, but to no avail. They thought she should go to a home where she would have attention. I knew Clara would have none of that.

Independent to the last, she stayed on at the old farm.

They die of loneliness, some say. Perhaps it's true, for in a matter of months, Clara joined her Albert.

On a beautiful July day, I found myself at the farm but with a heavy heart. The house seemed to sag a little more; the lawn was badly in need of cutting and the jungle had invaded the vegetable garden. All was quiet.

In my mind's eye, in cloistered shadow, I could see a ghostly figure bent low over the garden. I turned away for the last time. Some of my world had died - some of America had died.

WOMAN IN THE CORN

Mosey, Gotch, and I had been hunting in the scrub and pine near the lake and were now dragging ourselves up a dirt road covered by a light, early-morning snowfall. As we approached the main road, a small foreign car came along. Suddenly, in a cloud of snow, it hooked off across a shallow ditch then plowed into some standing field corn.

Luckily it came to a stop still upright. Being a scant 100 yards away, a short sprint brought us to the car in seconds.

There was only one person inside: a woman who sat motionless behind the wheel. Gotch opened the door and asked, "You alright, ma'am?"

For a few seconds she neither spoke nor moved. Then, haltingly, she said, "I . . . I guess I'm alright."

Mosey spoke. "Ya look a little peaked. I trust it's from the accident and not us. I assure ya we're civilized, ma'am; even though we have guns we're not members of the Mafia."

A wisp of a smile crossed her ashen face.

I said, "There's an emergency vehicle up in the fire barn and if you're hurtin' in any way…"

"No . . . No, I'm ok. I bumped my head slightly on the steering wheel, but it's nothing."

Mosey said, "Friend of mine struck his head in an accident a few weeks ago. He had an X-ray but they didn't find anythin' either way."

Gotch asked, "What do ya figure caused the car to fly off the road?"

She replied, "It could have been two things. Some drifted snow along the side of the road caught my wheels and turned me toward the shoulder. My brakes seem to grab on that side too. A few weeks ago I took the car in to have them repaired but they still don't seem to work right."

Mosey said, "Hard to get things fixed right these days. Seems like a lot of people doin' the fixin' ain't been put together right."

"I might agree with that," she said. "Right now, my problem is how to get out of here. Is there a towing service handy?"

Gotch answered, "Not nearby, ma'am, but I think the three of us can get that little car back on the road. We won't have to cross the ditch. When we get it out of the corn it'll be downhill less than 100 feet to the head of the lane we just came up. Once there we'll have it on the main road in no time. When Mosey gets his 225 pounds behind the car, I'm sure it'll move."

Mosey said, "Put her in reverse and tread lightly on the gas pedal."

She started the motor. Slowly and surely we moved it out of the corn and turned it around. Near the lane, the ground under the snow was soft and the wheels spun, throwing up some mud, but the car gained solid ground and was soon on the main road.

She got out of the car and, seeing some mud on Gotch's pants, said, "I'm sorry you got splattered."

Mosey replied, "He should have more sense than to push right behind the wheel. He's a half-wit, ma'am. In fact he's hardly got his paddle in the water."

"Those are hard words for a friend," she said.

Gotch replied, "Don't let it worry ya none, ma'am. He's been nasty like that all his life but we've become accustomed to it."

She said, "I'm trying to get to Cortland. Do I turn left at the corners just ahead?"

Gotch answered, "Ya could just go that way, however it would be about 22,000 miles before ya come around again and we set ya on the right track. Better go straight ahead."

She flashed a full moon smile. "I'm glad you fellows were around to assist me. Sometimes I think I'm over the hill - getting too old to drive."

Mosey replied, "You're a long way from being too old to drive, ma'am, but even if ya were up in years, remember it's better to be over the hill than under it."

She laughed heartily then reached in and took her pocketbook from the seat, opened it, and said, "I want to give you something for your troubles." Mosey was quick to reply, "You don't owe us a thing, ma'am. We're glad to help."

Gotch said, "We're content knowing you're all right and feelin' like your old . . . I mean young self. Take care, and if ya ever come this way again just remember ya can park in our corn field anytime."

She laughed and slid behind the wheel. The motor sprang to life and with a wave of her hand, she moved off up the road.

IT'S GOT TO BE A SUNNY DAY

I was at the town store feeding gas to my always-hungry car when Henty pulled up and slipped his husky frame from behind the wheel. He noticed me at the pump and shuffled over.

"Givin' some more money to those poker-playin' A-rabs, I see."

"Not that I like to do it, but I can't run the dang thing on aspirin tablets and Pepsi Cola," I said.

"It sure is a problem. At least we can do most of our heatin' around here with wood. Saves quite a bit of money and cuts down on oil use."

Thinking about the problem I almost pumped more gas than I could pay for. We went into the store. I paid my bill and we struck up a conversation again.

"Henty," I said, "It looks like you're pickin' up a little weight."

"It's true I spend too much time at the supper table. Should be doin' the chores."

"Why feel bad about it if your wife's such a good cook?"

"It ain't that at all. She talks a blue streak - asks so many questions I can't eat. Food ain't all that good anyway. Gave some of it to my dog the other night . . . sure broke him from beggin'."

Henty stared out the window and reflected on a landscape bathed in sunshine. "Wish I had enough time to do a little fishin' today. It would be beautiful on the lake. There's hardly a breath of air stirrin'."

I asked, "Do ya still keep that old rowboat on your frontage?"

"Yeah. In fact, that new neighbor of mine pestered me about goin' fishin' so much that I finally took him out a week ago to put a stop to it."

"Catch much?"

"No, but my good spinnin' rod passed on."

"How did ya manage that?"

"I didn't. My partner had trouble with his reel. I had another old pole in the boat so like a fool I handed him my good rod. About ten minutes later I found out the guy was a magician."

"What do ya mean he was a magician?"

"Well, he whacked my rod on the gunnel and made two poles out of it."

I broke up.

Henty thumped me on the back and said, "A lot of sympathy I got from you."

"It just proves one thing. You should only go fishin' with old friends like me."

"Maybe so," Henty replied. "Ya know, in my lifetime I've tried many things and stuck to just one -- fishin.'"

I thought I'd needle him a bit as I said, "Fishin' seems like an awful waste of time."

He smiled and knowingly said, "Doesn't bother me at all. I could fish forever."

"Don't ya want to improve yourself?"

He mulled that over for a while and replied, "I suppose I could take up fly fishin.'"

"To be serious for a moment - when did ya first go fishin'?"

"I can't remember that far back. My father told me once that as a baby I escaped from my playpen and crawled into the creek behind the house. Father swears I was trying to catch the brook trout with my hands." He paused for a moment and then continued.

"When I was a boy, after our long winters, those warm spring days were tantilizin'. I'd get rambunctious as the devil in school . . . lookin' out the window . . . hardly wait for the school day to end so's I could grab a pole and head for the creek. Ya know how the kids would bring apples to the kids? Sometimes I think the teacher offered me as many as three apples to go home!"

"I doubt it was that bad, Henty."

"Well, it ain't too far-fetched. My thoughts were often on green fields, singing birds streams, and if in my daydreams there was a surging trout on the line, all the better. As a kid I was pretty dumb.

There were times in my reveries when I couldn't find my classroom. In fact on some beautiful spring days when the trout were bitin" I couldn't even find the school."

I smiled and said, "Ya know Henty, I had a few days like that myself."

CURE FOR INSOMNIA

There is a multiplicity of problems these days, both physical and mental, that contribute to an affliction known as insomnia. Certainly it must be widespread when one views the TV commercials that concern themselves with sleeping aids.

In service years the other extreme seemed to be the case. Men were so tired that it was difficult to get them on their feet for duty. The usual procedure of shaking and shouting did not suffice and more severe measures were undertaken.

One night in North Africa near Algiers, a few of us were trying to arouse some men for guard duty. By prodding and rolling them around we got all but two awake. Those two had to be held, hands and feet, and were dropped several times before we got more than a grunt out of them.

Somewhere on the road west of Constantine I had an experience that made me understand the depth of weariness. I was seated close to the cab on one of the fold-down wooden seats that graced the army truck. My barracks bag was between my legs, arms folded on top and head resting on them. The left side of my helmet liner was propped against the wooden latticework that surrounded all but the small window on the back of the cab.

As I catnapped, the truck was bouncing around considerably on the bumpy dirt road and my helmet liner slowly worked its way toward the top of my head. I don't know how long I slept, perhaps 25 or 30 minutes, but when I awoke I found my helmet liner had slipped completely off and my head was making contact with one of the boards around the cab. Evidently the pounding had been going on for some time, because on the side of my head was a bump that resembled half a golf ball.

As far as land forces were concerned, the war in Africa was over when we arrived at Philippeville close to the Tunisian border. Here in a British tent area we were quartered. It was located in a sandy draw with dunes on either side, just a stone's throw from the sea. We arrived at dusk and no sooner had settled down that the rain began to fall by the bucketful. In the narrow draw there were two rows of tents with backs on the gentler slope at the foot of the dunes. We lay in the sand, heads on higher ground. Sleep came in seconds but we were rudely awakened in short order. The stakes pulled out of the sand and the tent slapped us in the face. By the time it was pitched again all were soaked but we quickly returned to slumberland and made it through the night without further incident.

On rising I was surprised to find that I had added several pounds. It seems the downpour saturated the sand until little rivulets formed. I was lying in one of the tracings and all night long while I slept, the water had been running inside my collar, through clothing, eventually trapping the water-laden sand in the bag of my pants formed by my leggings.

In Italy we found it easy to sleep through most anything, including air raids. One early evening, machine guns clattered, anti-aircraft guns of all descriptions joined the fray and bombs dropped - one about 60 yards away. We were in the basement of a building that had the back blown off by a previous bombing. The shock wave of the exploding bomb close by cracked the walls, pieces of mortar came down and dust from all four walls advanced toward the center of the room.

With the earth-shattering din of the raid over, the dust cleared. I glanced at a friend of mine who had been sprawled on his side on the tile floor about ten feet away when the fireworks began. He was still in the same position. I didn't notice any movement. Maybe he was . . . I rose from my sitting position with back against the wall and walked to him. Using the side of my foot I gave him a kick on the butt that rolled him on his belly. That evoked a low moan and a slow roll until he was on his back. Opening his eyes in stages, then staring at me for a moment, he said, "Luke, ya lousy good-for-nothin' . . . can't ya let a man sleep!"

THE LIFT OF FRIENDS

I was slidin' by Mosey's farm returnin' from my wood lot when I sighted him and Ginty sittin' in the side yard. I stopped and as I walked toward them, noticed their sweat-stained clothes. No doubt they had been hard at it, but I figured if I got them involved in a lively chat the result would only enhance the effort so I said, "If ya haven't enough work to do I can keep ya busy cuttin' wood."

"Hey," said Mosey, "Ginty and I just finished stackin' over a hundred bales of alfalfa in the barn, so don't give us none of your insinuatin' remarks."

I said, "Let's face it, you're loafin'. A few honest words can't hurt ya anyway."

"Well, I don't know about that," Ginty said. "One Saturday morning when I was a kid, things weren't goin' too well. In the first hour I had about a week's worth of trouble and, feelin' sorry for myself, announced I was goin' to run away. My brother ran upstairs and packed a suitcase. Mother made me a sandwich and father graciously opened the door. It was the fastest I ever saw the family move. Have I seen trouble from a few ill-chosen words? I've seen plenty."

Mosey interrupted. "Actually you're lucky, Ginty. Think of all the trouble ya would have seen if ya were sober most of the time. You'll be in more trouble, if ya keep answerin' your own questions."

Ginty took the barbs in stride and replied, "There's nothin' wrong in talkin' to yourself. Some doctors say it's healthy. Anyway I need to talk to a better class of people some of the time."

While I was thinkin' that one over, Mosey's son, Al, came out of the house, got in his father's car, and started up the drive.

Mosey hollered, "Where ya goin'?"

"To the store," Al answered. Mosey shook his head.

Ginty asked, "How's the new car runnin'?"

"Good, I guess. Don't drive it too much. There seems to be one thing installed in the car that I didn't pay for and it gives me quite a lot of trouble."

"What's that?" I asked.

"My son," Mosey replied. "He looks for excuses to drive. I think he took that evening class in pottery makin' at the high school just so he could get behind the wheel."

"How does he like the class?" Ginty questioned.

"All right, I guess, although last week he told me he cracked a few pots. I told him not to worry too much as there are a lot of crackpots on his mother's side of the family."

After I regained my composure I asked Ginty if everything was all right with his one-tractor farm. At one time he called it a one-horse farm but progress changed that.

He said, "Lately for some reason the cows have been a little jumpy at milkin' time. Thought maybe I had B.O. or somethin'. I put on some industrial-strength cologne but it didn't help none. There's another problem that's worse, however. My well water has begun to taste funny. I think sulfur is gettin' into it. I've come up with some intestinal trouble and I got a hunch that's where it's comin' from. Brings back the army days when the G.I.'s would hit every now and then."

He started to laugh.

"What's so funny?" I asked.

Ginty, now in control of himself, replied, "Reminds me of one of the inscriptions on the walls of Montezuma's Tomb. An archaeologist was tryin' to decipher it and finally he exclaimed, 'I've got it!' One of his coworkers asked, 'What does it say?' The guy replied, 'Don't drink the water.' That gives me an idea, maybe I should bottle my well water. Might be the best reducin' plan ever…could make a fortune."

I always feel better after talkin' with Mosey and Ginty.

ONCE THERE WAS A HEART

Two men sipped beer at one end of the bar while the bartender washed glasses. The hour was late. A shabbily-dressed figure, broom in hand, shuffle from the back room. Sparse hair did little to camouflage his baldness. Several days' growth of beard shadowed a blunt face. His faded blue sport shirt with the top two buttons missing, hung on shoulders that lacked muscle of another year. He stopped, leaned on the broom, then addressed the bartender.

"Finished sweepin' the back, Artie. Anythin' else ya want me ta do?"

"Ya might mop up that spill there."

He pointed to a spot on the floor where the fatter of the two at the bar had just spilled some beer.

"Why do ya keep that punch-drunk bum around, Artie?" the fat one said as he nodded toward Barney.

"He gives me a lift, earns a little spendin' money, and you want to remember he was a pretty good fighter in his day."

"Once, maybe, but he ain't nothin' now," said the thinner one.

Barney caught the conversation as he leaned on the broom, body swaying and head bobbing as if ducking punches from a phantom boxer.

"I beat a lotta guys, lotta guys, didn't I Artie?"

"Sure did," Artie replied and, sensing Barney's rising answer added, "Get the mop, Barney, will ya?"

"Sure Artie, sure."

He hesitated a moment, glaring at the two men, then drifted toward the back room.

Artie turned to the men.

"Don't get on Barney. He's a decent guy and not as harmless as he looks. He might just bust ya up."

"The way he's rockin' around now, I doubt he could punch his way out of a paper bag," said the fat one.

"Don't be too sure," Artie said. "Maybe he ain't in the shape he was when he took some of the best middleweights in the world, but just lay off him or ya might get a surprise."

"Ok, ok," said the fat one.

Barney returned with mop in hand and proceeded to wipe up the spilled beer.

A man in his late twenties, hatless, wearing dungarees and a jacket, entered the tavern and slowly moved toward the bar. He glanced at Barney, then his eyes swept the two men seated nearby. Arriving at the bar he pulled a small handgun from his jacket pocket and shoved it under Artie's nose."

"Open the register and give me the bills," he said.

Artie did not belabor the point. He quickly plucked the bills from the various compartments and thrust them in the man's outstretched hand. The man stuffed the bills in his pocket and headed for the door. Watching intently, showing little emotion, Barney released the mop and stepped into the man's path.

"Ain't gonna take that money from my friend Artie," he shouted as he lunged at the intruder, his left hand grasping the collar of the gunman's jacket. The gun roared. Barney recoiled but his hand still clutched the collar. The holdup man stared wide-eyed, expecting Barney to fall. Barney swung widely with his looping right and caught his adversary full on the side of his head. Down went the gunman, dead weight, pulling Barney to the floor.

Barney, bending low, finally released his hold, staggered up and with a forced smile, looked at Artie.

"Licked da bum, didn't I Artie?"

"Sure did, champ," Artie answered.

A low moan escaped Barney's lips as he pitched forward, dead.

ECHOES FROM THE OLYMPICS

The chant swelled to a roar ... "U-S-A! U-S-A!" It electrified every American within the arena and flooded out across the valleys and down the mountainsides from Lake Placid to quicken the pulse and lift the heart of a nation.

Game after game the United States hockey team rose to meet the challenge, facing formidable odds, denying victory to opponents. With each goal, flags waved, cheers cascaded down, and together team and spectators buoyed each other and took the giant steps down the road to what seemed to be an inevitable predestined final victory.

Some may have thought before the competition began that the United States team was a bunch of inept kids, but if that were the case they would never reach out and shake the tree and bring down golden fruit. They suffered from long months of practice and many games before the Olympics. Here, they did the things that had to be done whether they liked them or not. They developed the talents and powers that made them uncommon athletes.

When the time came, the disciplines were there . . . the character in each man that molded the character of the team. They were ready for the journey. Yes, they were schoolboys, in general having played for college teams, but men with skilled game.

And yet, who would think that such men could face professionals - for that is what some teams were - especially the Russians who had played together for years and had defeated National Hockey League teams as well as professional all-stars. So, the path to gold was lined with near-impregnable roadblocks. If adversity was to be overcome, it had to be faced, and one at a time they faced the roadblocks.

Each step strengthened wills, like making a piece of steel . . . a little heat and pounding. Resolute and determined, with the score against them, they rallied to the attack and endured the clash of battle. No talk of failure here. Devotion to excellence was a constant theme.

They scaled the heights of emotion, glorying in each others' plays like a blazing fire driving the shadows back. The tide rolled on . . . upset after stunning upset . . . the crowd responded, flags unfurled and spirits like an eagle soared.

Those within the arena were a catalyst expressing the genuine joy that slipped the bonds of all restraint and left in its wake all-consuming pride in team and country. It affected the multitudes watching on TV.

All the world gazed in wonder. It was a fresh wind that blew across the mountains and valleys from Placid. A wind that extended our reach ... lifted our hearts . . . enriched our lives. A great lesson for the younger generation – for everyone. All of us need a glory, something to hang onto, to fight for, and it was here. We were in need of heroes and they were in our midst. They allowed us to drink from their glass a tonic for all that call themselves Americans.

Americans enjoy seeing the underdog triumph against overwhelming odds, and our team gave us that satisfaction. They made a difference in people for the better and left as a heritage to those that follow some of the great lessons in life.

On that wonderful Sunday the golden dream was fulfilled. In the final victory all hearts were one. Unbraided joy in the proper setting, in the proper perspective. Players fell on one another and flags were paraded up and down the arena. The taste of it was clean and good.

The sight of goalie Jim Craig, with the flag draped over his shoulders, and Captain Mike Eruzione singing the National Anthem on the awards stand, made many an eye glisten.

I could hear a whisper . . . duty, honor, country. Five men proud of flag and all that is wrapped up in its fabric. A truer message could not be found.

The tumult at Lake Placid has long since died but the echoes will stand the test of time. The glory of their victory will live forever in the annals of sport and also in the hearts of their countrymen.

Still to my ears will come the chant . . . "U-S-A! U-S-A!"

THE GLORY OF THE GARDEN

The Great Depression brought drastic changes to lifestyles in my neighborhood. Many backyards became vegetable gardens. Also, tracks of land were rented by government agencies and then partitioned and doled out to those in need. My father was given a section and although it was over a mile away and we didn't have a car, we managed very well.

An old cart was garnered from somewhere and, with scrap lumber and boxwood, higher sides were built. We were now able to transport tools, pails, and whatever else might be necessary. The pails became a most important item the first summer because of drought conditions.

The garden was on a tract of land quite close to town with an old apple orchard on one side and on another a heavy growth of brush, saplings, and weeds. About 100 yards from the garden and in the brush was an old well with a bucket and rope handy. To keep the vegetables growing, the well became our salvation.

I was about 11 or 12 years old at the time and tried to do my part. The water hauling was somewhat of a problem. Using two buckets was better because it balanced the body. However, if you filled them much more than halfway, water would be spilled. Negotiating the rough terrain was like an obstacle course for me. One of my early trips was met with disaster. The garden path was about 20 yards away when I tripped and lost my valuable cargo. It was a sad, frustrating experienced and I moaned and groaned as I returned to the well. In short order I became cognizant of the obstacles to be faced when I was involved in the water brigade. The bucket's wire pails produced blisters that soon broke, causing hands to bleed. I managed to alleviate the problem to some degree by padding my hands with rags.

When we brought produce home, we had a long, steep hill to surmount. Only when we had a heavy load of potatoes did it give us trouble. Then, my brother and I would take turns pushing the wagon to make it easier on father, who was always on the pulling end.

My father boxed in one corner of the basement, making a cold cellar. It was about four feet high and above it were shelves. Potatoes, beets, and squash were stored there. Thanks to my mother the shelves were stocked with mason jars of tomatoes, green beans, chili sauce, and jelly made from wild blackberries.

The garden was a godsend that gave sustenance long after the summer months. In my mind's eye comes a vision of the three of us tending that plot of land, and to this day I am thankful for the loan of the land that made such a difference in our lives.

THE PAUL REVERE OF THE NORTH

Our camp was based on one of the large rushing rivers that run north to the coast of Quebec, near the Labrador border. A floatplane had dropped us to check the area for a possible fishing camp. We were up and about at an early hour. The sun crawling over the barren hills across the river was slowly taking the damp chill from our clothing.

A hearty meal was soon packed away and equipment, including fishing tackle, rain gear, plus a healthy lunch, was stored in the freighter-canoe. We moved steadily upriver for a few miles, then turned into a shallow bay where a small stream tumbled down to meet the quiet waters. The heavy canoe was pulled up on a patch of grass, packs were adjusted and, with fishing poles in hand, we started our trek across a large island that we had scanned on our rather sketchy map the night before.

The grass and bush soon vanished, giving way to a picket fence of stunted spruce trees. It wasn't as formidable as first appeared, however; even though some windfalls had to be stepped over, narrow alley ways carpeted with caribou moss hastened our progress. A woodland caribou was jumped and trotted off rather hurriedly. Then, the spruce trees thinned and all of a sudden, we were in a strip of grassland about a half-mile long and a quarter-mile wide. A few hundred yards away, a caribou grazed, not knowing we had intruded on his domain. He soon sighted us heading toward the safety of the forest. The grassland was quite marshy; still, it was easier walking, and good time was made until the trees closed in once more.

Some time passed before we broke clear and faced the other half of the wayward river. We dragged our weary feet over the large boulders that lined the shore. Here and there, we stopped to cast a lure and see what developed. This part of the job interested me most, as I never remember being forced to fish, and a respite from the long trek was most welcome.

Within the cold clear water, great numbers of lake trout, brook trout, and landlocked salmon lurked, and because they were often in the same pool, you were never certain what might strike, and situating ourselves on a large flat rock, we threw a few twigs together and brewed a pot of tea which washed down an ample lunch. We went back to pounding river again but all too soon, the fishing had to cease. If camp was to be reached before nightfall, our attention must be given to several miles of rock-hopping and bush travel that would have to be traversed before the canoe would ease us back to camp.

For a time, we retraced our steps along the river; then, feeling we could cut the hypotenuse of the triangle, we turned inland. Treading through caribou moss and then rising to the top of a rocky knoll, we got a line on the spot where we figured our canoe awaited us. Striking out again through the dense timber, we were plodding right along when we suddenly came to a small lake hidden in a saddle. I doubt it was more than 300 yards wide and less than a half-mile in length. We came in at one end and started down the shoreline when a sharp report from the direction of the lake snapped us to attention. All that met our gaze were circles radiating outward from a spot a short distance from the shore; either a very large fish or a beaver alerting the creatures of the wilderness.

Keeping watch on the lake as best I could without tripping over some obstacle, I soon solved the mystery. A beaver surfaced, swam a short distance, saw the stranger on shore, and again sounded the alarm. His tail rose high in the air and came down with a resounding crack. I don't know whether the beaver wanted to keep tabs on us or not, but he swam all the way down the lake closely paralleling the shore. Of course, most of the progress was made underwater and his pace matched ours so perfectly that each time he surfaced, we were right alongside. We were quite interested in him because we had never seen a beaver this far north; then, too, as time went by, our companion afforded us a few laughs. Each time he came up, he glanced shoreward, sighted the enemy and fired a shot heard round the lake.

Now, even beavers get tired, and after going through the ritual several times, he began to weaken. The first place it showed was in his large flat tail. It began to droop and the reports dropped to a whisper by the time we neared the end of the lake. Here, it stopped for a moment to see if he would surface for the last time. I wasn't denied his final appearance. He looked at me as if to say, "Are you still there?" Then, with great effort, part of his tail rose a scant inch or two and settled silently back into the water. I thought it was a pretty sad performance. I imagine he did too. No doubt he was happy to see us go. Even if he didn't enjoy my company, I enjoyed his, and as I trotted to catch up with the rest of the party, I was laughing so hard at the beaver's predicament that I tripped over a windfall and nearly went head over teakettle.

EPICUREAN ARTS - A LA ARMY

Did you ever taste something so bad that over a multitude of years the taste still lingers?

Through the courtesy of the army I was first introduced to "C" ration the day I landed in North Africa, and the last time I found it necessary to dine on the abominable stuff was in Italy in 1945. I didn't care for it then and nothing's changed.

We sat in the dust and stone piles of North Africa, dipping into cans of cold "C" ration with a mess kit spoon that resembled a tablespoon. Later on, from time to time, we had field kitchens and were then rewarded with hot "C" ration. It had one advantage over cold; the heat would melt the grease, thus allowing it to slide down the pipes a little easier. The army was right about one thing - "C" ration would definitely sustain life over some period of time.

Normally each meal of "C" ration consisted of two cans. One contained the main course, like stew or hash, and the other as I recall held three round, thick crackers, a few pieces of hard candy, and a small tin of either powdered coffee or chocolate. The crackers were really hard tack, which we called dog biscuits because they resembled dog biscuits in color and hardness but tasted something like animal crackers.

High in the Atlas Mountains on the narrow twisting road to Algiers, our convoy stopped so that we might enjoy one of those delectable meals. We sat by the side of the road. A few steps away, the sheer walls of a gorge dropped 1,000 feet or more and on the other side we could see the road that we had labored up about an hour before. Not having been overseas long, we were somewhat extravagant in our ways. One of the men said he could throw a dog biscuit across to the road on the other side. The dog biscuit sailed beautifully but fell a half mile short of the mark. Several men followed suit just to see the detested biscuits disappear into the abyss below. I fired one away but gnawed on the other two. Actually, I thought they tasted good, at least compared to the stuff in the other can.

I remember another fine meal the morning after we shipped out of Philippeville near the Tunisian border one rainy night and headed for Italy. We boarded a ship called the Champollion. It was an old, dirty, French tub run by an English crew. In the mess area they had tables that reminded me of the picnic variety with seats attached. Eight men would eat at each table and rations would be drawn by one man.

When mess call came I went to the galley to pick up food for my group and was handed two pails. I knew right then things were going to get interesting. There were two men behind the counter. The first one dumped in mustard pickles and the second, slices of bread . . . a half-bucket of each. I suppose you could call it breakfast but I didn't think too highly of it; neither did the men. In fact, after that delightful repast, I never had much of an appetite for mustard pickles.

A few years later I was on shipboard once again; this time heading home. Near Gibraltar we passed an aircraft carrier that was supposed to take us back but had been held up due to inclement weather. Late November on the North Atlantic was a notoriously bad time. Some of us may have been lucky because on its return run the carrier was damaged by tremendous waves and had three men washed out of a forward compartment.

Our ship was the Sea Tiger, a 12,500-ton cargo vessel. Without ballast the bow would come full out of the water, then boom and shake when it found support once again. The captain called the storm the worst he had seen in his long career. It held us in its grasp most of the way home and the men suffered the agony of seasickness. Perhaps they suffered more because of the lack of good food through overseas years. Few of us, if any, had tasted fresh milk, fruit, vegetables, or meat. Without refrigeration you live out of the can.

It was under these conditions that Thanksgiving of 1945 arrived. Below decks there was the stench of sickness. I was trying to get some air on the heaving deck when the meal was served. I had no inclination to eat but headed down, picked up a tray and small servings of turkey, dressing, and mashed potatoes, and ambled over to one of the stand-up tables. There was plenty of room; in fact, I was alone. I leaned against the bolted-down table and tried to keep the tray from sliding. For a moment I gazed at the best food I had seen in years, then took a bit of turkey and some dressing. It was all over, and I mean all over. I dragged myself up the passageway to the deck, sat back to superstructure, and prayed the wretched voyage would end.

As we approached the States, the storm lessened in intensity. By the time we reached New York harbor, ship and stomachs were on a more even keel and appetites were returning.

The Sea Tiger progressed up the Hudson River to Camp Shanks and here, human cargo disembarked to waiting ferries. As we moved shoreward, Red Cross women handed us cartons of milk, the first fresh milk since leaving the States. It was downed in fast order.

We were marshaled to barracks, where duffels were deposited, and after the luxury of lengthy, warm showers, gaunt weary men trooped to the mess hall. Compared to restaurant bill of fare, the meal may not have been up to bar, but to us with our advanced hunger for dairy products and fresh meat, it was exceptional. Moving through the chow line, trays were filled with containers of milk, a slab of ice cream, steak, and other accouterments. Later that evening, I wandered to the P.X. and added two milkshakes and a few pints of ice cream.

Through the late afternoon and evening I had consumed three quarts of milk and ice cream without ill effects and, as I climbed into my bunk that night, I was thankful to be in my own country again.

MOSEY'S DILEMMA

I was out front pruning locust trees when Mosey came by. That's not his name - it's Rutherford, but nobody calls him that because he's six feet, four inches tall and built like a bear. Actually, they call him Mosey because when leaving, he always says, "Guess I'll be moseyin' along."

"Ya know," he said, "a salesman stopped the other day while I was replacin' a few fence posts roadside. Slowed me down quite a spell gettin' stuck and bendin' my ear."

"How in heaven's name did he get stuck? We haven't had any rain in over a week," I said.

"Well, ya might say he worked at it. Pulled in the driveway and somehow got his right ear wheel over the end a' the culvert. With it resin' on air and the bottom a' the car draggin' anchor, he couldn't go nowhere."

"How did ya get him free?"

"The tractor came to mind, but thought I might rip some a' the bottom of his car so I used some planks and a jack."

"Take long?"

"About 20 minutes and all the time he was talkin' and I was workin'. The way he talks, the guy's downright overbearin'; got an answer for everythin', that is, except how to get his car out."

"Didn't do a thing, huh?"

"No siree. Not a blamed thing. But I didn't worry too much about it at the time. I jus' wanted to get rid a' the blow hard. Doubt there's much he'd be good at anyway, exceptin' maybe as social director on a garbage scow."

I laughed. "You're a little hard on him."

"Hard! Heck, you didn't have to listen to the guy. Even my dog couldn't stand 'im. He was lyin' there tryin' to get a little shuteye, and after a while he started growlin', so's I had to shut him up. Thought ol' Duke was gonna take a chunk outta 'im."

"How'd ya get rid of the pest?"

"I'll tell ya, it wasn't easy. You'd think he was one a them schizophrenes, or whatever they call 'em. He holds conversations with his self. Asks a question and before ya can open yer mouth, he answers it! I'd worry about 'im around the farm. If he ever fell in my waterin' trough, he'd drown for sure."

"Ya still haven't told me how ya got rid of him and what he was sellin'.

He laughed. "Fertilizer."

"Buy any?"

"No. Cows manufacture about all I need." He thought a moment and then continued. "I hope the guy didn't drown."

"What do ya mean?"

"Well, he told me how he knew a lot a people around here and was quite familiar with the territory."

"What's that got to do with drowning?"

"I'm gettin' to it. Hold your horses. When he finally got ready to leave he looked down the hillside and said, 'Where's the nearest bridge over the river?' I laughed and he asked me what was so funny."

"About then I couldn't help myself. He had jus' told me how much he knew about the territory so I thought I'd let him find out a little about the river."

"There isn't any river around here," I said.

"You know that and I know that but old 'know-it-all' didn't. From where we stood it did look like a river. The steep bordering hills and ridge on the hillside below my farm hides the near shore and a good piece a the lake. You've got to admit, it does look narrow."

"It may look narrow, but it's well over half a mile wide at that point. What did ya do?"

"Told 'im to head north and take the first left."

"Lord help him," I said, "that road's steep as the devil and if he doesn't make the last turn that hooks toward the cottages, he's gonna play submarine."

"Ya know," he said, "you're right." He laughed again and then added, "It's sure as shootin' there ain't no bridge or ferry boat and if he takes a notion to ford that little 'river' he's gonna find about 300 feet of water over his head when he reaches the middle. Skaneateles is pretty deep." He laughed till his whole body shook."

In due time he recovered sufficiently and with a wave of his hand, said, "Guess I'll be moseyin' along."

See? I told ya he'd say that.

Edwin Lukens

A MAN FOR THE TIMES

Gotch is a successful small farmer, which is saying a lot in these days of giants. It would be like Gotch to prove the little man still has a place in the scheme of things for he is a fighter and about as independent a cuss as one can find. Gotch is a tall 6'2" and thin, with a long nose and gray eyes -a real Ichabod Crane type. His spread is less than 300 acres and run with the aid of one other person, a son in his mid-twenties.

Farming is not a 9-to-5 business. A reversal of the figures would be a little closer to fact - from 5 AM to 9 PM. Hay and grain were raised, primarily corn to feed the herd of Holstein milkers which, in turn, provided income to keep the operation financially sound. Of course, all was dependent on the whims of Mother Nature.

Gotch had little time away from the land, but he did stop occasionally on his return from grocery shopping in town, or if he saw me around the yard as he was driving by on a tractor or other farm equipment. There were also times when I returned the favor. As the years passed, my admiration grew. A farmer not only drives heavy equipment as he tills and crops the soil, but he must be a mechanic, a carpenter, an electrician, and more. And Gotch was much more. He had character, molded in respect for the land and the fight to exist. Not one to rationalize in the solving of problems, he moved quickly to the crux of the matter. He was also somewhat of a philosopher and had a fine sense of humor.

We were talking a while ago about the energy problem, and Gotch figured he had a solution to the gas shortage.

He said, "I saw a demonstration on TV the other day. They had two cars goin' along, one at 55 and the other at 70 MPH. They made the statement that the one goin' 55 would save 25% on gas consumption. Now that set me to thinkin'. If 15 MPH less saved 25%, then three times 15 MPH less would save 75% more, which would be 100% savin'. You would be goin' 10 MPH without ever addin' gas. That isn't too fast but it's better than walkin'."

I laughed and said, "Did you try it out yet?"

He replied, "No, but I'll get to it one of these days."

Gotch continued, "I was standin' in front of the grocery store in town last week, talkin' to a few friends about this energy mess when Father Quinn came along. I mentioned I was gonna convert and he heard the key word as he approached. He said in surprise, 'Gotch, are you converting?' 'Yeah,' I said, 'from oil to wood.' He didn't say a word; gave me a strange look, then went on down the street."

One afternoon I was helping Gotch with some timber - not that he asked, mind you. We were using cant hooks, moving logs up an incline and onto a stake truck. As we stopped a moment to rest, I said, "You ought to be proud of this spread. You keep it in good shape."

He replied, "If it wasn't for that terrorist group I'd do better."

"Terrorist group?" I said. "What do you mean?"

"That outfit that really puts the fear of God in you. I think they call it the I.R.S." He added, "About the only thing I can afford is bein' poor. I guess that's somethin' my family passed on from generation to generation." He straightened, placed palms over the end of the cant hook handle for support and remarked, "When you think of it, we're privileged. In some countries I'd be lucky to have a handful of rice for daily sustenance and in others I might be workin' for the state, givin' some if not all of what I produce to the government."

I knew Gotch couldn't be serious for long.

He reiterated, "Yeah, about the only thing I can afford is bein' poor. Of course, I've got an excuse. I came from a broken home. When I was 7 years old we had a hurricane. Porch blew off."

When I regained my composure I said, "Gotch, I think you missed your calling."

"You may be kiddin' but actually I think of that quite often. Sometimes I really doubt I found my callin' . . . I can still hear voices."

I ducked away from him and remarked, "I imagine you hear a lot of them."

He didn't throw the cant hook at me but in a serious vein said, "I couldn't leave this farm. They say the man owns the land but more often it's a case of the land ownin' the man."

He gazed at the surrounding countryside for a moment. I broke his reverie by changing the subject.

"Do you ever hunt that thicket along the stream for partridge?"

"Oh . . . now and then. I'm not too successful. You've heard this old proverb: A bird in the hand is worth two in the bush."

He winked at me as he added, "Sometimes two in the bush can be mighty interestin', though!"

I FIND A DAMSEL IN DISTRESS

IT was a bright, brisk October day, one that would satisfy any man. Just a whisper of breeze was mixing the red and yellow leaves in a stand of maples that bordered the patch of scrub apple where I worked partridge.

As I shuffled along, hopeful of getting one of the small, feathery projectiles airborne, the movement of a much larger creature to my left caught my eye. From behind a clump of small maples a scant twenty yards away, stepped a tall, striking woman. She carried a twenty-gauge, double-barrelled shotgun, and was nattily dressed for such an occasion. Suede shoes, plaid slacks, a red sweater with the sleeves pushed up above the elbows, and a suede vest graced her slender form. I regained my composure and smiled as I moved toward her. She was a very beautiful woman, bronzed by many suns, with dark hair trailing down in a ponytail. I was armed, yet disarmed, at the same moment.

We chatted for a few minutes, and in so doing I learned that she was lost. I also found out, much to my chagrin, that she was married. Nevertheless, who deserts a lady in distress?

She had left a little red sports car, and her husband, about a mile back on a dirt road. He set out to climb a hill on one side of the road while she turned toward the woods in the opposite direction. Why they chose this arrangement I'll never know. Perhaps they were afraid of shooting each other.

I was only a few hundred yards from my own car, so I offered to take her on a tour of the surrounding countryside in search of the little red car. Surprisingly enough, she accepted my invitation, and as we worked our way toward my car, I gleaned more information to fit into the puzzle.

The only dirt road in the area, other than the one my car was parked on, was a mile to the east across a small stream. We arrived at the car, and after situating ourselves, moved north on the dusty, winding road. Soon, we crossed a bridge over the stream; then, turning abruptly, headed back in almost the same direction as we had come. My lovely companion sat quietly, looking intently from side to side in search of familiar landmarks. None seemed to evoke a rise out of her. Finally, as we came out of a shallow bend, a gleaming red Corvette caught my eye. My friend nearly went through the roof as she screamed in delight. I pulled to a stop. She alighted, smiling, thanked me twice over, and bid me farewell.

I had to admit I enjoyed her company. I hunted another area for a time, but without any luck. My mind didn't seem to be on partridges. Driving home, I smiled inwardly as I recalled the events of the day. It was pleasant to know that a woman could enjoy hunting and the outdoors. I admired her greatly for this, and for one other reason: she was the second of two beautiful women who could look at my ugly face, and smile.

WHEN LEAVES TURN IN LABRADOR

I stumbled out of the tent into morning air with a deeper chill than before, and eased down the steep riverbank to wash and remove the last vestige of sleep from my drowsy head. Struggling back up the gravelly incline, made more difficult because of a towel dancing around my wet face, I paused at the brink for a moment to survey the majesty of the wilderness.

Alone I stand, and yet I am not alone. The sentinel of the north, a lonely White-Throated Sparrow, accompanies me with friendship and song, as he flits from bough to bough in the tag alders that border the riverbank.

The river's thin veil of morning mist breaks clear, while just below me in a dark, sleepy pool, a brook trout jumps high in a glistening shower of spray, returning to his friendly haunts with a resounding slap.

Early fall leaves float by on the river's edge, leaves that burst forth in color just before their deaths.

Already joining ranks for the flight south, a flock of ducks circle and I hear the whisper of set wings as they drop in to pay their compliments. Entranced, I watch them paddle about, parting the water like little boats with feathery bows.

I raise my eyes to the far shore where sun sifts through the tops of spruce trees. The fragrance of evergreen is everywhere. A sea of dark green breaks away from shadowed water, rising up gradual slopes of low-lying hills topped with stands of white birch, now blazing yellow from nature's magic touch. Well beyond, above a purple haze, fleecy white clouds crown dawn-shining mountains. A young breeze gentles birch leaves; it dies, and from a roaring rapid, hushed by miles, comes the river's ancient song, still strong through a thousand years.

In the early light I stand, and in the far distance comes again the White Throat's song. A song soon stilled by winter's icy hand.

THREE STREAMS OF YOUTH

Thomas Wolfe wrote a book entitled, *You Can't Go Home Again*. In my mind's eye, however, I can penetrate the shadowy curtain of the mounting years and once again capture a passing parade of bright memories. A constant pleasant theme encompasses three laughing streams whose clear, cool waters meant so much to me when I was a light-footed lad.

In two of those streams, the last trout has swum to oblivion and, if the third provides any fishing, it must be near the headwaters, for most of it serves as little more than a drainage ditch. But in my youth, the crystal waters gurgled over graveled bottoms and swirled around roots of verdant vegetation that shaded much of their length.

Harbor Brook was the first to enter my life. It was readily accessible, being little more than a half-mile from my house. I fished it regularly from Velasko Road to the second bridge upstream, spring and summer, in search of brown and brook trout.

From Velasko to the bridge near Marble Farms, stately elms lined the banks and many a quiet pool provided a savory meal. As a youngster, I assumed it would never change.

When the elms were cut down and the stream dredged, it was goodbye forever.

I turned my attention to Stolp's Gulley, for that's what we called it; most people knew it as Furnace Brook. West of Elmwood Park to the falls above the site of Corcoran High School became more familiar to me. In a short time this, too, changed. The valley was timbered, houses built, and in the streams last days, the runoff from heavy rains caused the fish to die of sand-gills. Also phosphate levels increased until the stream became choked with algae.

The third stream entered my world - Geddes Brook. It was a long hike from home but young legs are strong and almost tireless. In quest of trout I trod the timeworn paths along its banks from Genesee Street to the headwaters some two miles away. The stream meandered through pasture land, scrub willow, and hardwoods. Wildflowers grew throughout the valley. In spring, adderstongues, trilliums, hepaticas, and many other varieties blossomed in gay profusion. With all the beauty for the eye to behold, still the added bounty - trout.

Some favorite spots will intrude forever on my mind... the imprint clear to the minutest detail; the eye of back eddies and undercut banks where darting fish came to the hook.

One pool in the upper reaches straddled a sharp ravine. A log jam at the base held back 40 feet of water. At the head, water primarily from two springs ran swiftly over a smooth shale bottom then fell a few feet into a deep pool. there was little water beyond the springs and no roads close by upstream. If anyone were to stumble upon it, they would come from the opposite direction. However, one other problem presented itself. Below the pool, the stream dropped abruptly over a rocky bed; a raceway for 200 yards or more, with few if any holes that would hold trout. I imagine some fishermen bypassed the past water and found my little paradise, but if they did, no human stain was left behind.

Presently, the area stands as a monument to progress. A shopping center and a few hundred houses cover the landscape. At least I am content in my memories, for I knew the streams when nature held sway and the inroads of civilization had yet to scar the land.

SECOND OPINIONS

In many fields of endeavor, second opinions are the order of the day. I could be called gullible I suppose, but it's more a case of trust. I like to believe in people, so I have a habit of thinking words spoken are the truth. From time to time, I get a rude awakening.

I dealt with an antique dealer a while ago and was told that most of the articles in my possession were of little value. Six dollars was received for one item that I noticed had a forty-eight dollar price tag on it when I later visited the store. It seemed to me that if it was worth forty-two dollars more than I was given, maybe the payment could have been somewhat higher. I do not wish to cast aspersions on all antique dealers, as I have dealt with some, including two brothers, who play a different game. They are fine, decent men who have become good friends of mine.

Words of Wisdom

In the medical field - specifically when it pertains to surgery - second opinions are of great importance. I have a good friend who was a prominent surgeon. I say was, because he is now retired. He adheres to that principle concerning second opinions.

I went to a psychiatrist some time ago and, after checking me out and asking lots of questions, he said, "You really are crazy." I replied, "I'd like a second opinion." He said, "Okay, you're ugly too."

That was not the second opinion I have been referring to. And then again, in my case, maybe I needed a third opinion. Anyway, when a situation calls for it, don't hesitate to get a second opinion.

II. COACH LUKENS

Edwin Lukens

WESTHILL HIGH SCHOOL MOVING UP DAY SPEECH, 1977

As you know, I rarely wear a tie. However, on this wonderful day, certainly an auspicious occasion, I wish to honor the students here assembled, so I wear a tie.

I hope my words this morning will not embarrass you. I trust you will tolerate me as I wander from time to time.

Let me go on to things of a more positive nature. This school of ours is a household of learning. Some people may have a mistaken idea of the function of a school. It makes a contribution to people. It exists to serve the needs of people, to extend man's reach, to lift his heart, to enrich and ennoble his life. The duty of a school is to see that each student committed to its care preserves and develops his or her freedom, special powers, and individuality - the maximum development of the individual.

Yes, the purpose of Westhill is to make a difference in people.

To make uncommon people, not common ones.

Most important, fine, decent, reputable citizens.

Here you have a chance to rise, to excel. There may be some who don't try to rise or excel. They may be afraid of defeat. But failure often spurs success. The better the character the stronger the effort.

Remember too, you can fail at something every day and still not be a failure.

Don't limit acceptance of life by feelings of unworthiness.

I have used that old adage -- if at first you don't succeed, try, try again. To baseball players - if at first you don't succeed, try second base. TRY - SOMEPLACE!

One of the great inventive geniuses of past years, who invented (among other things) the self-starter for automobiles, put it another way: If at first you don't succeed, fail again. Now that sounds strange, but he added another line. Don't fail the last time you try. And that's the way it is with inventors. Fail a hundred times, but on the next attempt, hit the jackpot. It takes a lot of discipline to struggle on in the face of adversity. And that discipline, I trust, comes in a constructive way from parents, administrators, many others, and that includes teachers.

Of course, when it comes from teachers, it's mantled in deep self-respect. Actually, when we can stand on our own two feet and govern our words and actions with good, uncommon, Onondaga Hill or Westvale horse sense, then we have true character which comes from this self-discipline. And you know, perhaps the most valuable result of all education is the ability to make yourself do the thing you have to do, when it ought to be done, whether you like it or not. It is the first lesson that ought to be learned, and however early a person's training begins, it is probably the last lesson that is learned thoroughly.

Let me tell you a little story, but first let me preface it. This school is for you, not teachers, administrators, and all personnel connected with the education process. And that means everyone.

A school is not a floor, four walls, and a roof. It's the human element that counts. Now, on to my story.

One day, as I travelled through one of the glass corridors, I overheard a girl sitting with two others remark, "This school stinks." Now that's a profound statement. Using the same vernacular, I stopped and said, "Why does it stink?" Well, she hemmed and hawed, but never came up with anything of a positive nature.

So then I asked her if she was involved in any of the school activities like band, chorus, drama club, sports program, or what have you.

She said she wasn't, and that to me was the crux of the problem.

I plead with you to avail yourselves to the opportunities that exist. Get into the mainstream of life at Westhill. You learn about life by participating in it.

There are so many venues of study, from core curriculum, to design, art, photo, car mechanics, and so on; and, of course, the aforementioned extra-curricular activities. We cover many facets of education. Again, stick your foot in the door, reach out to unexplored corridors, or you will never realize your potential. As one fellow put it, "Shake the tree of life and bring down fruit unheard of." And further, getting involved in activities will lead to a sense of belonging. You will become part of the school and therefore a better citizen of school and community. That means pride in school, and pride in self.

I've often made the statement to physical education classes, and especially to athletes, that I have been privileged to coach. Making a man is like making a piece of steel. It takes a little heat and a little pounding. If adversity is to be overcome, it has to be faced. Continually walking away from it or rationalizing does little to develop character - and speaking of character in another light, moral integrity.

My grandfather once told me, "The closer you come to a mud puddle, the more chance there is of falling in." Something to think about. And you know, when it comes to values, old-fashioned ones are still in vogue. A few years ago it seemed everybody was protesting something or other; concern or injustice or inequity of all walks of life is fine. Many it seemed were protesting just for the sake of protest - no remedies to alleviate problems. Some even wanted to destroy all the guideposts of the past, but if you do, it may well be that you will destroy the foundations of the future. Nothing can be built on ashes.

I would admit to more than a little anger when I watched the flag desecrated on TV. Patriotism doesn't have to be worn on your sleeve, but what's wrong with a quiet, deep, reverence for our flag and its meaning? It stands for all that has transpired in this country, good and bad. But I believe most was good. Wars have been fought, most with just cause. All that were wounded, paid the supreme sacrifice. Framers of the constitution, presidents, Presidents like George Washington, Abraham Lincoln, Teddy Roosevelt, and a peanut farer by the name of Carter. And advances in medicine - think what the polio vaccine did for mankind. I would elaborate on that theme, but I'll leave that to you.

There are those who scream "freedom!" but deny it to others. Within the rules and regulations of school and law of the land, you have great freedom. And I would wish you all the freedom that is compatible with good manners, ethical conduct, and family honor.

Some of my greatest satisfactions have been with young people and that includes members of the graduating class. I thank them for their many kindnesses, and for their many struggles and accomplishments in Westhill's name.

As for the athletes who are graduating - your challenges of future years will be battles of a more subtle nature and yet of lasting duration. Many will be tougher and I implore you to direct those energies once utilized on the friendly fields of strife to good advantage in years to come.

The tragedy of life is what dies within a person while he lives.

And all of us need a glory, something to hang onto, to work for, to fight for - the enemy is surrender.

To all the graduates - society needs men and women of your caliber who add to our immediate world and enhance the future as well.

To all the wonderful students in this gathering, allow me to recite this little poem:

> You are better than all the ballads ever sung or said;
> For you are the living poems,
> All the rest are dead.

Rather high-sounding words, but true. You are the lifeblood of Westhill, of community, yes, and country.

Well, you and I have been through a lot of blood, sweat, and tears together. Let me say something about the other side of the coin. To those that put their hearts and souls into the seemingly all-encompassing tasks of the day - responsibilities, considerations. You have well earned a respite, a time to enjoy.

I leave you with this comment, made by one of the great athletes of his time, to a young, aspiring athlete who had just had a temper tantrum.

The younger fellow later became one of the greatest in the game, by the way.

The old veteran put his hand on the young man's shoulder and said, "Don't hurry, don't worry, you're here for a short visit; take time to smell the flowers."

Please, take time to smell the flowers.

Thank you.

JUST A COACH?

It is often said that a coach can fashion a workable unit from relatively raw material. If this cooperative and coordinated effort can be attained, it should follow that he can mold the honesty and moral integrity that is so necessary in this day. Without high ideals, athletics is a journey never completed. Within the athletic program lies fertile ground for great moral growth. It also can be ground where a multitude of sins deleterious to the well being of the athlete can be perpetrated, and in fact infect in a chain reaction multitudes down through the years.

As a manufacturer may turn out a shoddy product, so can a coach. The coach, by setting high standards, develops character within the athlete by his own leadership. Whether he realizes it or not, he projects part of himself into his charges. Winning is not to be frowned upon. This country was built on competition. However, failure to teach in a way that stresses the principles of honesty and moral integrity are stressed to a great degree would be a grievous wrong. On the other hand, if the standards are high, never to be strayed upon, they are beacons that will illumine the lives of generations yet to follow.

When the last whistle blows and the last shout dies upon the hills, how will you be judged?

WELCOME BACK

[Editor's note: this undated article about Ed Lukens was included as a testament to his legacy as a coach and an educator.]

Coach Lukens spent a few evenings this year with former students. Mandana's Tim Cowan had an agenda for his class reunion this year. As a member of Syracuse's former Central High School's class 46 years ago, he was charged with making sure Coach Lukens got an invitation. Ed Lukens, a former gym teacher and coach at Central, was well remembered by his former students, so much so that they not only wanted him to share their reunion but also to honor him. They did this in a big way with a letter from George Bush.

Dear Mr. Lukens,

Congratulations on your years of service as an educator. American's young people rely on our educators for the knowledge and guidance they need to succeed in school and in life. By building the minds and character of our country's youth, teachers enrich lives and inspire students to achieve their full potential. Your hard work and dedication reflect the spirit of our Nation.

Laura and I send our best wishes. May God bless you, and may God continue to bless America.

Sincerely, George Bush

Lukens said he was flabbergasted. He had been thrilled to just be invited. His former student Andris Kalnins commutes to the White House every day. He had issued the invite, spoken to the President and paid for Lukens' dinner too.

About 100 former classmates gathered at the Kirkville fire department building where Lukens was singled out for his impact on his former students.

Lukens is a resident of Borodino (28 years) and a veteran of World War II. He was in North Africa and Italy as an infantryman.

After the war he attended Syracuse University where he was honored as a Letterman of Distinction in track and field. He was a hurdler and a long jumper. He also threw a javelin.

He is in the Syracuse Sports Hall of Fame is also a senior's master athlete who still holds several world records in track and field events.

Two additional Central classes invited Lukens to their reunions this year. The message was the same: As a coach he was inspirational not only in his pursuit of excellence in athletics but also in how ones plays the game. In addition, how this translates to everyday life.

ONE LUCKY COACH

Many years ago, I was privileged to coach a fine track team. They swept through the league invitational meets and the State III Sectional championships with ease. In the section meet, I missed an outstanding athlete because his father had to make a job switch to New Jersey. It was the middle of his junior year and he wanted to stay with an aunt and graduate here. If this problem had come about halfway through is senior year I might have said yes, as it would stem any disruption in academic or athletic endeavor at a crucial time. So it was sad to see him go for more reasons than one, but I was sure it was the right decision. If he had been a member of the team in sectional competition they would have swept almost every event.

In his senior year, at Easter time, he came into town. He climbed over the wall and barbed wire that surrounded old Archbold Stadium to get to the discus area. Here we worked to iron out his turn. In the New Jersey State Championships he took that event and two others. Did I ever miss him.

Mentioning this team in such a favorable light might give anyone the idea that I had an ego, but this is not the case. Credit for the wonderful performances that transpired along the way belongs to the athletes who were well beyond the normal in ability and also in their understanding of the world around them. They were not boys but men concerning the qualities that mold strength and unyielding character.

Victories were sweet, but that is not the real story. The real story is the one that lay beneath the surface. It had to do with the dogged determination, dedication and perseverance that would not be denied, come hell or high water. The facility where the team practiced was the worst one I had ever seen in my lifetime. The track was a misnomer. It was a raised area around a football field that had been a bicycle track in the 1800s. The distance around it did not measure up to track standards and the surface was irregular, stony and even had glass on it from time to time. On rainy days, the weight men would kid about the shots disappearing in the mud. There was one pit for several events where we tried to keep a wealth of sawdust.

Once, when the park custodian was not around, I sawed two limbs off a maple tree because I feared my pole-vaulter might disappear in the tree. To hide the evidence, the limbs were cut up and stuffed in my wagon. We had one vaulting pole and it was locked in the park field house but it did not take long for the door to be smashed in and a pole stolen. All other track equipment was kept in my wagon. That includes a fork, rake, blocks, batons, shots, discs, measuring tape, medical supplies, etc.

As a coach having seen a multiplicity of facilities, I cannot comprehend why team members did not fill the air with thunder concerning the extremely rotten conditions that prevailed. Actually, alibis were nonexistent. They did not use conditions as an alibi for lack of performance. There was a constant unwavering effort toward personal and team goals. Being the rock solid individuals they were, existing conditions only released greater energy as they moved ever forward. They gloried in accomplishment and passed it on in the camaraderie that permeated the entire team.

There was another problem that might have stopped students who were thinking of coming out for track. It was a mile or so from school to the park. Books and equipment had to be lugged and when practice was over many walked a mile or two home. Others picked up a city bus a quarter mile away, transferred downtown and rode another two miles to their destinations.

The metric system was not utilized at the time this team existed. On the team was a fine 16-year-old junior half-miler. In the state meet, he was boxed on the last turn and as he came off it, he had slow, swing outside, then print to the finish line. He missed first place by about a foot but if he did not have the problem, he might have won in about 1:55 and that would be excellent time.

Here, the story takes another twist because that fine athlete spoke to me about a desire to go to Yale and possibly complete his senior year in prep school. I sent letters to a few top-notch schools and Philip's Exeter Academy offered a scholarship for that year. Some people might wonder about my action. I was comfortable with it, although I missed him for many reasons. Sometime later, he told me his freshman year at Yale was relatively easy after prep school. He had a good career at Yale and then went on to Columbia Medical School. He is presently a surgeon in Nashville. I received a letter and card from him this past Christmas. To hear from these men out of the past is my greatest reward.

Long ago, I was involved with a fine team. I thank heaven for the bright memories that won't let go, of their wonderful performances under terrible conditions and circumstances. It is a parade that will forever march through my mind. It is more than athletic endeavor that took place in that crucible where defeat seemed everywhere. It was a game of life. They faced adversities at every turn, yet gained the higher ground.

LUKENS' FAREWELL TO SENIORS AT WESTHILL HIGH SCHOOL JUNE 9, 1978

I won't use any Hollywood superlatives, just let me say simply, and honestly, it is indeed an honor to be invited here and I trust I can leave a message that might be of value to you.

Perhaps it's good to take a look at the past to reminisce, as concerns Westhill and hopefully what has transpired there.

Soon you will be heading out into the world, possibly to further education or to a job. In truth, education never ceases. If you wish to make a better world, it's good to have the material ready. That's what school is about, academics, school activities, sports, all are facets of the educational process. Training is everything; cauliflower is nothing but cabbage with a college education. It is good to have a wide range of interests, rich background of service, of responsibility, of accomplishment, maybe we could use the word consideration along with responsibility.

Consideration for family and friends – here, we build trust and respect. It is important to look good in other people's eyes, but even more so in your own. Be true to the light within. Teachers should let you stumble occasionally. Parents should too, just to see if you can right your own ship and stand alone. Tolerate parents and teacher; remember they're not young enough to know everything. Enterprise and character will take you as far now as in the past. Enthusiasm, alertness are still noticed and appreciated, at the same time you can still cut yourself off from the pervasive conformity, vulgarity, hysterical clamor and other corrupting influences around you. You have a choice, and there's still plenty of room for people who want to be left alone.

Certainly discipline is one of the pillars of character. One of the old Roman philosophers, Cicero, had something to say on this subject. He said, "When the method and discipline of knowledge are added to talent, the result is usually altogether outstanding." I think a certain connotation can be arrived upon – that being the meaning of work, of practice. Often we hear the word "perfection." Really I doubt anyone ever attained it. The danger does not lie in failing to reach perfection, it lies in giving up the chase.

Actually, when we talk about the quest for goals, the true measure of living is not the acquisition of money or power or reputation. It is awareness. The intensity of awareness is one of the greatest gifts. Therefore you should never feel guilty for seeking out places or experiences where this awareness might be found. If anything, the guilt lies in not searching for them more eagerly and more often, for no one has unlimited time.

Let me digress for a moment... one of the saddest, most terrible things that ever happened to this country was the Great Depression. People eventually worked their way out of that dark hole. A disaster converted by many to an asset; disasters can be stepping-stones to success. One man said it was the worst despair a nation could undergo, short of invasion by an enemy, nothing will ever be worse than this, if we can climb out we're home free, and nothing has been worse. Challenge unleashed dormant energy, what opportunity existed awakened sleeping talents; hardship brought forth unsuspecting courage and endurance, and the freedom we have enabled people to grow to full stature. In school there should be the challenge of achievement and conversely, the penalty of failure; also the reward for striving and always the avenue for liberating energy in constructive ways.

A moment ago I mentioned courage. A Greek philosopher, Plato to be exact, said courage is wisdom concerning danger. Spirit of fear destroys, cripples, distorts. Many people are best when scared or when a challenge is thrown at them. In the face of this difficulty or danger, you learn to trust yourself. Often it is fear that spurs people on. Fear, rightly used, is the father of courage. Be thankful for challenge, it makes you do your best. Some, however, don't meet challenges. They rationalize; actually, we're all guilty of it from time to time. I could do it but -- I've used that line and so have you. The important thing is that we attack problems positively most of the time.

People who bring many problems upon themselves overwork this expression, "No one gave me a chance." The truth usually lies in the statement, "They never gave themselves a chance." Certainly there will be outside influences, but by and large your life will be what you make it. The responsible, reputable citizen is to be congratulated. Certainly the one that doesn't meet these standards is dead weight and has to be carried by others. Many things we accept, but there are some we should not accept, waste of energy, crime in the streets, and drug problems. We can fight them; they can be changed for the better. As for the drug problem, if you have enough pride in yourself and want to function to the best of your ability, then why let something control your faculties?

Often you hear the expression, "Do your own thing," and I believe in doing your own thing, but if it means word or action that isn't conducive to the well being of others or especially yourself, then doing your own thing is crazy to say the least. Health is the most wonderful possession. If parents think enough of you, they will say no to certain requests. When they don't say anything, let you do as you please, then you have a real problem. It might be said, always do right; this will gratify some people and astonish the rest.

Let me add another piece of philosophy. You've heard the expression, "moderation in all things." A timeworn phrase and yet, if you take it to heart - believe me, it is a time-tested phrase, a worthy one indeed. Enough sleep, nutritious food, plenty of exercise. You won't enjoy your waking hours unless you get enough rest. Be alive - don't count the years, make the years count.

I hope what you have done at Westhill dictates to some degree what you ought to be, what you can be, what you will be. This struggle is the rally point to build courage, to regain faith, yes, to create hope. Finally, I trust we have built the aforementioned character that will mold you for your future roles as custodians of this nation. Don't relegate yourselves to mediocrity. There are too many social butterflies, with no concerted dedication to tangible or ideal ends. They show neither character nor appreciation. I think it best to ask a lot of yourself and you may be pleasantly surprised at how much you receive. Also, it is a good way to make friends and everybody can use friends.

Edwin Lukens

People grow old by deserting their ideals, years wrinkle the skin, but to give up enthusiasm wrinkles the soul.

I would hope for you, there is the love of wonder in each and everyone's heart gathered here, amazement at the stars, the undaunted challenge of events, unfailing childlike appetite for what next, and the joy of the game of living (the greatest game on earth). You are as young as your faith, as old as your doubt, as young as your self-confidence, as old as your fear, as young as your hope, as old as your despair. So long as your heart receives messages of beauty, cheer, courage, grandeur, and power from the earth, from man and from the infinite, so long you are young. When the wires are all down, and all the central places of your heart are covered with the snows of pessimism and the ice of cynicism, then and only then are you grown old indeed, and may God have mercy on your soul. Live everyday as if you expect to live forever.

As I look around a realize the great potential in this graduating class, I feel certain there is not a person here but has in his power to leave as a heritage to those that follow, the grandest thing on earth - character. There is a lot of room in this world for each and every one of you. So don't despair. You have been tolerant of my ineptitude. I shall remember you always.

Take care of yourselves!

God Bless You.

III. SONGS

Edwin Lukens

I STOLE A GEM

Verse 1:
I stole a gem from a valley town,
Came to the hills a higher ground.
When I turn homeward all things blend.
I find you waiting at journey's end.

Chorus:
When all our dreams are past and gone
And autumn leaves turn color on,
And time to say our last goodbye,
We'll be together, you and I.
(end only) We'll be together, you and I.

Verse 2:
You made my world a world sublime
Held me forever in the hands of time.
You took my dreams, didn't let them fly.
My love for you will never die.

Chorus

Verse 3:
Through sun and shadow, with you there,
No trouble will be hard to bear.
With never a hill that I can't climb,
You gave to me a life in rhyme.

Chorus

THE BLOOM OF THE ROSE

Verse 1:
One love may have slipped away
There'll always be another day.
Let no one tear your world apart
There's plenty of love for each heart.

You see girl, there's a forked road ahead
All that matters seems forever dead.
But don't ever think that life is done,
For he won't be the only one!

Chorus:
For you, it's spring just at the great,
Plenty of time to find a mate.
Wounds will heal, that door will close;
Comes once again the bloom of the rose.

Verse 2:
Now life isn't always a great ride;
Yet round the bend is a sweet side.
You may find a love like mine
That'll last you till the end of time.

Remember your heart is just on hold.
Love can yet come in from the cold,
Believe me, I know, I'll tell you true;
It happened to me, it can happen to you!

Repeat chorus

Edwin Lukens

LAST OF THE COWBOYS

Lyrics by Ed Lukens, Music by Ronnie Bell (1997)

Chorus:
If I could get a leg over this ole horse o' mine
"Just give me a boost, Lord, I'll only ask one time."
Then us two could ride out under an endless sky
I'm the last of the cowboys, I've got to say goodbye.

Verse 1:
You know fer shure, my last bronc's been rode
'Cause all through my life, I lived by the code
Been true to my buddies when we were drivin' cattle
Lord, I don't have much, just a horse and a saddle
Off to battle

Chorus

Verse 2:
I think of those who've ridden here before
Like the others, I will trouble you no more
A piece of me perished when I lost Ole Jim
Pushed by angry steer over the canyon rim, how grim

Chorus

Verse 3:
I've helped in tamin' this rugged and beautiful land
With fine cowpokes, a downright loyal band
Think twice on it, Lord, before your vote is cast
Put me in green pastures or down in Devil's Pass, at last

Chorus

ANNABELLE

Verse 1:
I took an empty road to nowhere
Leading down to cities' snare.
Away from you nothing but sorrow;
Let there be a sweet tomorrow!

Now past dreams just flood my mind,
Dreams I cannot leave behind.
It was your love that set me free
From the boy I used to be.

Chorus:
Take me to that higher ground,
Where laughter and love abound.
Please be there with open arms,
Oh greet me, Annabelle!

Verse 2:
Some might call it yesterday
But it's too many years away
Lovely visions of your face,
Draw me to that time and place.

Down a dusty road I chose to roam,
Measured steps now bring me home.
Rainbow, sweep the gloom away,
Show me where my heart will stay.

Repeat chorus

Edwin Lukens

WAKE THE ROSE

By Ed Lukens and Ronnie Bell
(1997)

Verse 1:
Whether near or far from home,
Doesn't matter where I roam,
You are always by my side,
Life is one fantastic ride.
Early morning. rising sun
Getting darker, nearly done.
You are always in my heart
We will never grow apart

Chorus:
Wake the rose
Wake the rose

Verse 2:
Walking by a river strand,
Crossing golden meadowland
Harmony is in my head
Giving love a brand new bed
Turning back the hands of time
Counting memories in a rhyme
Catching lightning in a jar
Reaching for my shooting star

Chorus and out:
Wake the rose, wake the rose
Catching lightning in a jar
Reaching for my shooting star
Wake the rose, wake the rose

Verse:

C min7, F min7 alternating

Chorus:

E min7, D min7 (flat 5), E min7, C min7

C min7, F min7 alternating C min7

Made in the USA
Columbia, SC
16 October 2017